RISEHOLME

PRACTICAL EVENTING

*Tinks Pottinger from New Zealand on Graphic, in fine
style over the Zig-Zag at Badminton. Cross-country
riding requires perfect harmony between horse and rider
if every fence is to be met and jumped well*

JANE HOLDERNESS-RODDAM

PRACTICAL EVENTING

Photographs by Bob Langrish

DAVID & CHARLES
Newton Abbot · London

I would like to thank Sandra McCallum and Pam
Cary for all their help and hard work with the
typing of the manuscript for this book. Also Judy
Cordy, Darrell Scaife, Cindy Collier and Kate Eld
for their help with the photography, and Bob Langrish
for his patience and superb pictures.

British Library Cataloguing in Publication Data
Holderness-Roddam, Jane
   Practical eventing.
   1. Riding competitions
   I. Title
   798.24

   ISBN 0-7153-9328-6

Typeset in 11/13pt Bembo by
ABM Typographics Ltd, Hull
and printed in Great Britain
by The Bath Press
for David & Charles Publishers plc
Brunel House Newton Abbot Devon

Contents

Introduction 7

1 The Sport 10

2 General Care of the Horse 24

3 Fitness and Basic Training 44

4 Jumping 68

5 Cross-country Riding 88

6 The Competition 112

7 Further Training for Horse and Rider 129

8 The Three-day Event 147

9 Coping with Common Problems 165

10 Helpful Hints 184

Conclusion 195

Further Reading and Useful Addresses 196

Index 197

To Our Nobby *and* Warrior *who between them won two Badmintons, one Burghley, one Olympic team and one European team gold medal, as well as numerous other prizes. Also to the many other horses who have carried me safely round several other one-, two- and three-day events, giving me such wonderful rides and exhilarating memories over the last twenty-five years.*

Introduction

Eventing is a tough sport, certainly not designed for the faint-hearted. Determination, the will to win, being able to work hard, general physical fitness and a reasonable standard of riding are some of the most important attributes.

Eventing, or horse trials as it is also called, can be likened to the pentathlon, only it is confined to horse sports: consisting of dressage, cross-country, and show jumping. The control and elegance required for dressage, where a test of set movements in sequence must be performed from memory in front of the judges, comes first. This is not easy for a horse who is also fit enough to run in the equivalent of a marathon. Tact, sympathy and patience are often stretched to their maximum, as the rider coaxes his mount through the various movements maintaining the degree of lightness and obedience so essential for good marks in this phase.

Dressage tests are designed in such a way that the basic training of the horse is demonstrated through the movements required. As the horse progresses through the ranks more will be expected of him, so it is important that the rider keeps thinking ahead to the next stage.

Cross-country riding is probably the rider's favourite phase. A course designed to test ability over solid, fixed obstacles at speed requires good judgement, training, ability and suppleness if all is to go well. The fences may include numerous problems requiring certain techniques to be used on certain types of fences. Again the severity of this test will be governed by the standard of the competition, especially as regards heights and spreads. In two-and three-day events this phase is preceded by a speed and endurance section, where the competitors cover marked distances to prove the fitness of their horses and a steeplechase course to show that they can gallop and jump at speed.

The last phase, show jumping, or stadium as it is called in America, is designed to test the horse's neatness over a course of coloured fences which knock down. A bad jump here can really put you out of the competition so a clear round makes all the difference between winning and losing.

*Cross-country riding at its best —
horse and rider sailing on over this
substantial hedge confidently and
looking ahead to the next fence*

Generally, competitions are designed as training for the ultimate aim – the three-day event. This is every eventer's goal but the training and knowledge required takes some time to acquire and the horses need a great deal of fitness, training, and time spent on their build-up to this goal. This book sets out to give a practical guide on how to achieve this goal, what is actually involved, what is required from both horse and rider, and how to set about the sport as a whole.

CHAPTER 1

The Sport

HOW TO GET STARTED

Eventing is one of those sports that can be started early in childhood. Because of its varied nature small children can be learning the basics in the Pony Club of all phases – dressage, cross-country and show jumping – or just specialising in any one of these activities at various competitions. It is a sport at which young people can really let off steam and 'go for it', but at which older people with the right temperament, nerve and ability can still win. Horsemastership plays a very big part and a brilliant rider with little knowledge of the physical capabilities and limitations of the horse will rarely stay at the top for long. A thorough knowledge of horses and riding is really what is required, so the sooner that this is learnt – and it only comes with experience – the better.

While many of the world's top riders have worked their way up from the bottom there is definitely a new generation who have not started competing seriously until well into their teens, and unless they have the benefit of good training and guidance at this time they often appear and disappear as 'flashes in the pan' who have become disillusioned when things go wrong and the pressures build up.

Some riders who have previously specialised in one aspect of the sport such as dressage or show jumping get bored and start to branch out into eventing, enjoying the varied training for the different phases that is vital for success.

In Britain there is a wealth of training available. The events themselves cater for pony riders, Pony Clubs and Riding Clubs, and cross-country schooling courses are appearing everywhere. Show jumping and dressage competitions take place throughout the year

---

The expertise of Ginny Leng and Nightcap is clearly demonstrated as they pop out over this big hedge, and turn in the air towards the next fence. Once experienced and confident, saving seconds in this way makes the big difference between success at the top and just missing the 'big time'

Training for the big time at a hunter trial, Mark Phillips demonstrates to perfection the essential softness of the hands and balance which make a jump easy for the horse. Four times winner of the Badminton Horse Trials, Mark has been one of Britain's most successful riders and now concentrates on writing, training and commentating throughout the world

and courses, clinics and lectures on the subject are organised endlessly. Events for all grades to compete in are regularly available virtually throughout the year.

In America a well organised competitive system exists but perhaps there is generally less chance than in Britain to compete in as many different competitions to build up the necessary experience. However, generally riders receive more basic training as it is normal for everyone to compete under the watchful eye of their trainer, who has carefully planned their programme for the season. The more general riding experience you have, the better, and those who have been lucky enough to have ridden racehorses, hunted, and team-chased as well as learnt all about getting horses fit for strenuous competitive work will all have gained a wonderful background to excelling in this thrilling sport. This and the following chapters aim to highlight the basic principles necessary to take you through the grades of eventing from one- to three-day level in as easy and practical a way as possible.

WHAT THE SPORT INVOLVES

Horse trials, or combined training as it is called in the USA is a sport that involves the most thorough all-round training for horse and rider. It is a type of equestrian pentathlon involving dressage, cross-country riding, speed and endurance including a steeplechase course, and show jumping. This must all be done with the same horse with penalty points being deducted for any errors in the dressage, any jumping faults or if the optimum time is exceeded. Although these are separate tests the penalty points are cumulative.

There are three main types of horse trials. The one-day event is the simplest and is the base from which most qualifications are built. It consists of a dressage test, cross-country course and single round of show jumping. In Britain this is usually carried out on the one day but in America, where such great distances are often travelled to get to an event, it tends to be spread out over a couple of days or more. The one-day event is designed as the training ground for every rider's ultimate dream – riding in a three-day event. It is a chance for horse and rider to progress and gain experience at the different levels without subjecting the horse to the stress of a full-blown three-day event. One-day events are divided into classes catering for the different standards of horse competing. Every country has its own national rules which vary slightly according to local needs. There is a grading system which enables horses to progress through the sport once a certain number of points has been achieved.

The two-day event is designed to give horses and riders experience at the various levels so that they have an idea of what to expect when they reach the three-day event. This consists of dressage and show jumping with the cross-country section extended to include modified steeplechase and roads and tracks phases. It is normally spread over two or more days and includes compulsory veterinary inspections. Two-day events usually cater particularly for riders and horses at the lower levels who are aiming for the three-day events.

Here we see Ian Stark and Murphy Himself making this big drop fence at Badminton look easy. Horse and rider are in perfect balance; the rider is sitting back and allowing the horse to use his head and neck. Note the security the rider has in his lower leg and heel. This is a beautiful picture of perfect balance between horse and rider

The three-day event is what horse trials are all about and is the ultimate goal for all event riders. The three different tests take place on separate days with three compulsory veterinary inspections being held at the start of the competition, before the cross-country phase and preceding the show jumping phase, on the last day. The first day (or sometimes this becomes two days if there are a lot of starters) is confined to dressage. The second day consists of two phases, A and C, of roads and tracks, with a steeplechase phase B in between; then a veterinary check and 10 minute compulsory halt to refresh the horse before the main phase D takes place round the cross-country course. On the last day the horses are presented for a veterinary check before finishing the competition over a course of show jumps. This is designed to test the horse's ability to continue actively after the demands of the previous day.

The three-day event is not only a test of riding skill but also one of horsemastership and the rider's ability to train the horse to the required level without unduly stressing the animal in the build-up to such a competition. Three-day events are normally run to cater for all, from those at novice or preliminary level who are just starting up to those aiming for international honours.

In Britain there are four categories of class. Pre-novice is for horses without points. Novice is for horses awarded less than 21 points, intermediate for those with 21-60 points and advanced for those with 60 or more points. The courses for these different grades have strict rules on heights and widths of fences, varying distances for the different standards and dressage tests designed to suit the horses competing.

In America there are five categories of class: novice, training, preliminary, intermediate and advanced, with Young Riders also being catered for. Horses are classified as follows: unrated, those with less than 10 points; Grade III 10-39 points; Grade II, 40-99 points; and Grade I, over 100 points.

RULES

Each national federation has strict rules on how the sport should be run and it is sometimes quite surprising how these can vary from one country to another. For instance in the USA penalty zones round each fence exist in all one-day events, as required under the International Equestrian Federation (FEI) rules for three-day events, but in Britain these only appear for three-day events.

Children aged 14 and four-year-old horses would certainly not be allowed to compete in Britain in official horse trials but at novice level they may do so in America. Most children compete in Pony Club events or as juniors for the European Championships. The latter's equivalent does not exist in the Americas although there is good provision of Young Riders classes for those aged from 14 to 21.

Whatever side of the Atlantic you are eventing from, it is well worth looking carefully through the rule book so that you do not run the risk of misunderstanding rules or regulations governing your sport. Each year most federations run an annual general meeting or general assembly when ideas are exchanged and decisions taken. It is important to keep up to date with what is going on within the sport and to send off registration or membership renewals in plenty of time before you wish to enter your first event of the season. Vaccination certificates and any other requirements should be checked in plenty of time, and any vaccinations that are necessary given early enough to ensure that your horse is fully over any side-effects before important competitions in which you hope to compete.

THE FEI

Whatever standard of competition the national federations run in their own countries, the international scene is run by the International Equestrian Federation (FEI) which organises and arranges the calendar of all these events worldwide. It also arranges for a grading 'star' system so that all three-day events classified as a CCI. (*Concours Complet Internationale*) are graded according to their standard. A one-star event (★) is expected to be roughly equivalent to a large preliminary or intermediate course suitable for horses just reaching international standard. Two stars (★★) are for horses with some international experience. The course will usually be of advanced standard without asking too many difficult questions, but may be quite big. Three stars (★★★) are for experienced international horses, and riders can expect to find a big and technical course. The most famous three-star events are Badminton and Burghley in the United Kingdom.

The FEI lays down all the rules for the international events, approves certain officials and judges who have to be chosen from its offical lists, and also lays down some qualifications for horse and rider.

In every event competitors are aiming for the individual classification, but sometimes there is an official or unofficial team classification run in conjunction with this. At World, Olympic, Continental and Regional Games (CCIOs) the team competition is hotly contested by the top nations. Four riders make up a team, but only the best three scores count. Teams of three may be entered but all members must complete to be considered. Teams are made up of members of one nation in championship events but in smaller events with unofficial team competitions mixed teams are sometimes made up to add interest.

The international calendar clearly shows the popularity of the sport and it is encouraging to see a steady increase in the number of countries taking part, despite often incredible difficulties in getting finance or expert help to improve their standards. The top nations are undoubtedly Britain, America, East and West Germany, New Zealand, France, Australia, Ireland and Holland, but Poland, Canada,

Spain, Korea, Italy, Russia, Belgium, Austria and Sweden along with many others have all produced some excellent performances that have proved how much talent there is within the sport.

THE RIGHT HORSE

Successful event horses come in all shapes and sizes and at the lower levels it is possible to have a lot of fun without having to worry too much about the breeding and type of horse required. Careful schooling, average jumping ability and the right attitude will get one a long way. There comes a time, however, when the right type of horse for this demanding sport should be thought about and the following points are worth considering.

How far are you aiming to go? At pre-novice to intermediate, or training to preliminary at one-day events the demands are not

Partnership is what it's all about, and these two seem to be getting along just fine. It is nice to see a horse going well in a simple snaffle bridle. The rider is giving her horse freedom with the upper part of her body. Her lower leg really needs to be a little further forwards, with more weight in the heel

excessive if the horse has been prepared conscientiously. However, if a three–day event is in line it is important to look at your horse and judge whether you really think he has the right build, conformation and breeding to stand up to what is undeniably a tough sport.

While it is sometimes possible to ask a generous horse to push itself occasionally further than perhaps it was ever designed to go, it is much better to have the right type of mount for horse trials in the first place.

Breeding

Breeding plays an important part. It is generally accepted that the three–quarter-bred or thoroughbred is the ideal with perhaps up to one-quarter other type to add a more calming influence to temperament. The thoroughbred can sometimes be too quick and sensitive, especially if not handled with understanding, but it has the desired stamina and speed. The addition of a bit of Irish blood, pony, warm blood etc, has often proved highly successful.

The temperament plays a very important part and this, combined with that of the rider, may be the whole secret of success. A brilliant jumper that simply will not settle in the dressage arena is going to become very frustrating so a calm, settled horse rather than a nervy and excitable type will definitely be more suitable. Find out a bit about the sire and dam if you can, in order to see what sort of horses they have produced.

General Conformation

Conformation should be looked at carefully. A well put-together horse with a good sloping shoulder should help to produce good movement and galloping ability. The horse must be deep enough through the girth so that there is sufficient room for heart and lung movement. A horse that is deep here is usually tough whereas the very shallow type tends to a lack of stamina.

Starting with the head and neck, the eye can tell one a lot and giving yourself a chance to study this as the horse is being shown off will help give an indication of the type of horse at which you are looking. Look at the head and ears: does it have a bold outlook and give the impression of courage and purpose? A pretty head is not generally liked on a competition horse, nor is one that has a definite 'bump' between the eyes as this is often a sign of stubbornness. The neck, which must be in proportion to the rest of the body, should be long and nicely arched, coming out of the middle of the back with a good curve into the throat on the underside. The back should be strong and well muscled. The quarters, where the main power comes from, should be well muscled and rounded and strong between the hind legs.

The limbs which are going to have to stand up to the demands of the sport are perhaps the most vital part to consider. The horse should stand four-square with the impression that his weight is evenly distributed on four well shaped feet. These should be tough, rounded and of matching pairs. Dark feet and legs are favoured, especially in front. Look at the knees and fetlocks or ankles; these should have strong but flat joints with short cannon-bones where the tendons stand out and are clearly defined. The overall picture should be one of balance and one pleasing to the eye.

Movement

Having assessed the horse standing still, it is then important to see it move. Look at the walk: does it take decent long strides and not go too close or too wide apart, especially behind? Run it up in hand and check

Mark Todd and Charisma in the dressage arena in the 1988 Olympics, where they won their second individual gold medal. Both horse and rider are extending the trot across the diagonal. The event horse must be bold and brave across country, but must show first that he is obedient and supple in the dressage

its movement again. The trot should be flowing and supple and the horse should move reasonably straight when viewed from behind. Those that swing a leg badly or turn a foot inwards are obviously going to be more prone to knocks or strains. The narrow-chested horse may also move very close. All this should be taken into careful consideration.

The feet are, of course, one of the most important factors of all and should be of a good shape, strong and tough. A concave sole, well grown heels, a strong frog and tough walls will all help but do check feet very carefully. If necessary talk to your farrier. The saying 'No foot no horse' is very, very true – many a brilliant horse has never reached its potential because of difficulty over shoeing or keeping shoes on a weak foot.

Having thoroughly investigated your horse it must never be forgotten that the right animal will only be a success if it is matched to the right jockey. This assessment is vital. Size plays a major role and while the ideal is probably 16-16.2hh this very much depends on the type of horse; whether it is a strong ride; the size, strength and ability of the rider; and whether the rider will have regular help with the horse. In Britain riders tend to do a lot by themselves, going for help only when necessary, whereas in the United States most riders are regularly under the guidance of a trainer throughout their careers and so have help from the start, often even with choosing the horse in the first place.

Final Assessment

The most important factor of all is your first overall impression – do you like the look of the horse, his outlook, his attitude to work and his temperament? Is he easy to do in the stable, in traffic – this is important, especially when you want to start him off on slow work to increase his fitness – does he 'hot up' in company, will he be capable of a good test, is he an athletic jumper who is neat and careful, particularly in front, when doing so? Can he gallop and does he look the tough hardy type suitable for the sport? Be quite confident that he is capable of these things, even though he may not at the time be sufficiently well schooled or educated to demonstrate this ability.

Always have the horse vetted to ensure that in a professional's opinion he is basically fit and healthy in eye, heart, wind, limb and general make and shape. The vet's report will also act as a certificate for insurance, should you decide on this, if you send it straight off to your insurers at the time of purchase. Vets will sometimes raise points about a horse that may affect your decision to buy. Few horses are ever 100 per cent in every way but the important point to discuss with the vet is whether in his opinion the horse is fit to do the job intended, or if any special precautions should be taken.

TRAINING FACILITIES

Having found the right horse it must then be given the right training to prepare it fully for the eventing scene. For this you need to have access to suitable fitness areas, a flat schooling arena or field, jumping facilities and cross-country fences.

For fitness roadwork is considered the basic essential, especially in Britain, so quiet roads suitable for the hours necessary to build up basic fitness are a priority. Hills are an added bonus, especially long gradual ones. Very steep ones tend to strain a horse, especially in the early stages of fitness training. In America and other countries where the climate is hot and the ground hard, roadwork is not considered so suitable as jarring tends to be a problem and therefore long slow hacks are more usual for this phase. If it is necessary because it is hard, cold or icy, slow work in indoor arenas is a good substitute but care must be taken not to overdo the horses in the unnatural going.

Once the horse's basic fitness is completed, groundwork to train for dressage and jumping starts. A large flat area is required. A proper training arena or school is the ideal but if this is not available a flat unrutted field or part of it will do. Arena boards or poles can be placed to indicate size and are essential to train your horse to do certain movements correctly before performing a professional dressage test. In fact as you get nearer to having to ride a dressage test practising in a proper arena really does become necessary, so if you have not got one yourself be sure you can have a few practices in someone else's.

Jumping training requires enough poles and standards or uprights to be able to erect a useful grid and some combination fences, with which to school as and when needed. For this you should reckon on having a minimum of twelve standards and sixteen to twenty poles with a gate, planks, wall etc as useful options, unless you can have the use of someone else's fences. Whatever your situation, poles or cavaletti are very useful training aids and can be put to numerous different uses.

For cross-country schooling you will need to find somewhere that you can take your horse for experience over combinations, bounces, corners, banks, and water obstacles as well as ditches in their many different guises. For this to be really beneficial it is best to be able to practise under instruction and over fences that will increase your and your horse's confidence. Therefore they should not be too big but of the size suitable for your and your horse's level of experience and standard.

For conditioning and galloping work good ground is essential, and if there is the added advantage of a hill (which should not be too steep) you are very fortunate. Very often a special gallop can be made with a little extra care of the ground such as regular harrowing, rolling etc. The addition of a few loads of peat, shavings, sand etc can often turn an adequate gallop into a very good one.

For some people the worries of whether they have, or have access to, suitable training facilities will not apply as they will already be with trainers who have all the necessary. However, for those thinking of taking up the sport and doing it from home, training facilities are a very important factor to take into account.

TRANSPORT

Transport is probably one of the most expensive aspects of the sport. You have to take your horse to the events, probably involving hundreds of miles of travel and hours of driving, so a comfortable, safe conveyance is vital. Whether you get a small or large gooseneck with the very useful pick-up truck towing it, a horsebox varying from the very smart down to the basic cattle-truck, or the little English trailer on the back of the inevitable Range Rover or whatever, it must be fully roadworthy, legal, safe and well equipped for both horse and driver for the journey to be undertaken.

This, of course, is very pricey especially by the time the vehicle is taxed, licensed, insured and filled with fuel for the season. The only comforting thought is that if you hired one for the season it would all cost considerably more!

THE RISKS

Eventing is an expensive sport and the very nature of it means that there will inevitably be casualties. Not necessarily from falls or injuries, which can happen anywhere along the line, but perhaps more from those who cannot take the long struggle to the top – and it can take a long time to get there. Also it is often not until you reach the advanced stage that it becomes apparent that the 'superstar' horse you thought you had is, in fact, unable to cope mentally with the bigtime and proves at best unreliable and at worst ungenuine. Many is the time that a brilliant one-day event horse proves to be no good at all, either for physical or mental reasons, when he reaches a three-day event. I once had a horse who was quite brilliant at home and everyone, from top trainers to top riders, thought he should be the next World Champion – but sadly this was not to be. Put him in a crowd and he just fell apart completely! I had a total ducking at Badminton once when he jumped into the lake; he was so busy looking at the crowd that he forgot to unfold his legs, so we both went under!

On the other hand, so often the horse you have despaired of ever achieving a thing at one-day events becomes a real hero at three-day level, excelling over the speed and endurance phases to move right up the placings. Our Nobby the little horse I rode at the Olympic Games in Mexico, never won or was ever higher than third in a single one-day event yet was fifth at his first attempt at Badminton, won it the second year and was third both years at Burghley – the only three-day events he took part in apart from the Olympics.

Even if you are lucky enough to acquire a horse that does have what it takes to reach the top, this does not mean that you will actually get there because it is the partnership that counts. It is just as important that *you* possess the right qualities as it is for the horse. While successful riders vary in size, make and shape, it really is their competitive spirit coupled with determination, the ability to communicate with the horse, a certain skill at riding at speed with accuracy over the cross-country, and with the capacity to command sufficient control and obedience for the dressage and jumping which tends to help win the medals. That essential quality, the will to win, helps enormously and certainly many a moderate rider has overcome all and succeeded in getting to the top through sheer determination and hard work. Others, such as dual Olympic Gold Medallist Mark Todd and triple European Champion Ginny Leng, have a natural in-built talent which is rare to find. For them winning is the norm rather than the exception.

CHAPTER 2

General Care of the Horse

The basic care of the event horse is one of the most essential factors in planning for success. How it is looked after, shod, fed, conditioned, trained and generally prepared for the season is at least half of the battle. The other half is a combination of the horse's own ability with that of its rider.

The event horse needs the usual good care and attention which every horse deserves. It should, however, be remembered that eventing is a tough and rugged sport and that to overcare for the horse is almost as bad as not caring enough. While routine is of course important do not allow this to take over as a priority, because the event horse has to compete at all sorts of different times of day during his career and in many instances may be ridden three or four times a day at one-day trials and combined training events. DO NOT always ride or school your horse at the same time of the day, but do try and stick to a feeding routine as much as possible.

Work out a practical programme for achieving your aims and then look at your programmes for fitness and training, and at the competitions in which you intend to compete. Decide on an achievable outline at the beginning of each season, with a few different options in case of problems along the way. There are always times when things go wrong, sometimes depressingly badly, but there should be the good times as well. Always be open to advice and if things have gone wrong try to assess why and when this happened. More often than not it's a little thing that leads to the bigger problems. If you can learn to spot these early and nip them in the bud before they develop into something major, either mental or physical, you will save yourself a lot of often unnecessary hassle.

WORMING

Every horse carries a worm burden but this can be successfully controlled by maintaining a regular worming routine. Your vet is the best person with whom to discuss the type of treatment and doses to

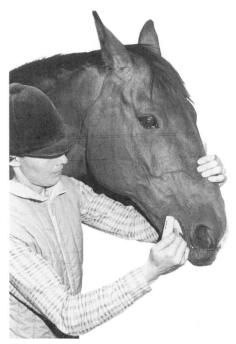

Administering a wormer

use. Remember there are several different sorts of worm, some being more prevalant at certain times of year. Redworm, bots, tapeworms etc are all extremely debilitating and for any horse to reach peak condition it is essential for worming to be conscientiously carried out.

When buying a new horse or acquiring one from another stable it is well worth getting a worm count taken and giving two good doses three weeks apart to correct any build-up if you feel the horse's previous owner was lax over this. Lack of condition and 'starey' coat, a big belly with poor top line, can all indicate the presence of worms.

Worming is an essential part of the horsecare routine, and should be carried out every four to six weeks. All horses have worms to a certain degree, and the belief that stabled horses are free from worms is both ignorant and naïve. Check that the brand of wormer used is effective against all the general types of worm. No horse will compete successfully unless in tip-top condition, so be sure to carry out a regular worming programme.

So often people forget the general rules of horse management, and cannot understand either how their animals do not look right, or fail to maintain condition. With regular worming and feed care this is most likely to be caused by an unsuitable feeding routine.

TEETH

Another equally important hazard to general health and wellbeing is sharp teeth. Not only does this affect the horse's ability to masticate its food properly, which in turn can result in poor digestion, but it can also badly affect the horse's way of going. Sharp hooks on the teeth can cause soreness to the cheeks and often to the tongue, resulting in head shaking, sucking up the tongue and erratic behaviour.

Teeth should be floated or rasped at least twice yearly, preferably by a horse dentist or specialist. Any unusual eating habits or fussiness in the mouth are usually connected with teeth. Wolf teeth, which develop in young horses, just in front of the molars, can be very uncomfortable when a bit is used. They should be removed and the horse given time to recover before wearing a bridle again. It is essential that the whole tooth is removed and that it is not broken off at the roots, which can happen if extreme care is not taken and will make matters even more uncomfortable than before. Be sure to study your horse's mouth for problems very thoroughly and regularly.

FEEDING

Having now ensured that the horse is able to chew its food and does not have a worm problem, the type of food given for the work it is doing needs careful assessment. The best criteria of success are whether the horse looks and feels healthy, is good in its coat and is working happily without becoming stressed. There are few hard and fast rules, except that it is quality rather than quantity that counts and all food given should be of the highest quality. Remember the horse is a herbivore and in its wild state would be nibbling as and when it felt nature intended. Within reason it is best for it to be able to eat hay ad lib – unless it is particularly greedy, in which case give small amounts at intervals. Fresh clean water should always be freely available.

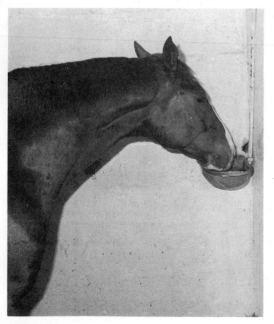

Automatic drinking bowls are labour-saving, but you cannot ascertain if your horse is taking his normal amount if, for example, he is ill. They should always be positioned in a corner where they will be out of the way, kept clean, and checked regularly to ensure they are refilling effectively. Most horses will quickly learn how to use them, but it is sensible to leave a bucket in the stable as well to begin with.

Automatic drinking bowl

Some horses require very little, others much more. At the Mexico Olympics my little horse Our Nobby, a tiny 15hh thoroughbred, and Richard Meade's 17hh Cornishman were fed very differently. Our Nobby had precisely 2lb (900g) of corn because I could not hold him on one side, and yet despite two falls he achieved the second fastest round in the speed and endurance phase. Cornishman had 22lb (9.9kg), and also did a fast round without mishap. Both were extremely fit and well for the last day. I do not intend to go into the art of feeding as it cannot be learnt from books and varies so much around the world, depending on climate, the time of the year and the degree of fitness of the horse. However, you should remember that mistakes are, more often than not, made through overfeeding rather than underfeeding. The build-up of such things as excess protein can be highly detrimental. What the horse needs, as we do ourselves, is a balanced diet. Giving too much of one thing and not enough of another can be disastrous, as can giving too many additives or supplements. Modern research has ensured that most mixes contain all the essential vitamins and amino acids vital to the horse's wellbeing. Also you must remember to introduce all food gradually and increase quantities over a few days. As the horse gets fitter the bulk roughage foods need to decrease and the energy and protein foods to increase. Remember that the ratio of bulk to concentrate should never drop below 40 per cent (bulk/roughage): 60 per cent (concentrates).

The conventional items such as bran (which should only be fed in moderation except as a mash once or twice weekly); oats, which are still the main source of protein and energy and the food of choice for fit competition horses; maize and sugar beet, both high in energy as well as fattening; and chaff, which adds bulk and helps the digestion, form some of the basic foods. Barley is fattening and less heating than oats, and is sometimes a good substitute for a 'hot' horse. It is best fed 'micronised' but should not be given in large amounts to the competition horse.

Flaked maize is a useful fattening food. Nowadays it is used less on its own but usually forms part of the 'mix' rations.

Sugar beet pulp and nuts are widely used as beet has a high energy and fibre content. Great care must be taken to ensure the pulp or nuts are properly soaked: they should be soaked in a bucket of water for at least 12 hours. They will expand anything up to three times their original size. NEVER feed unsoaked sugar beet as it has and will kill a horse if eaten before soaking.

Sugar beet, before and after soaking. This must be soaked in water in a 1:3 ratio for at least twelve hours before being fed. It is high in energy and a useful feed for all horses, but should only be given in moderate amounts or it may cause filling of the legs and looseness

Most horses love sugar beet and it is normally fed in 8oz–1lb (225g–450g) amounts after soaking. Occasionally you may find the odd horse which will get filled legs or become very loose on this food, in which case stop feeding it to that horse as it obviously does not suit the animal. Some horses will react in this way to a certain type of food and it is always best to cut it out and find a substitute if necessary.

There are various compound foods in the form of nuts or pellets, which are graded according to the amount of protein they contain. Extruded food is the most recent improvement to animal feeding; the food is broken down through a heat process and so is more easily digested. Less is necessary and digestive problems are reduced to a minimum. Most of the leading manufacturers are now looking towards this process.

Very popular nowadays are the various mixes which contain all the essential foods in a balanced formula. Most horses like these and they are produced in a variety of types to suit the different levels of work, from those doing competition down to ponies just hacking or out at grass.

Samples of typical foods given to the competitive horse, including good quality hay, oats, barley, maize, bran, chaff, sugar beet and nuts. The quality of food and the way it is fed plays a major role in how the horse builds up condition. Every horse must be treated as an individual and fed accordingly

Molasses is another highly nutritious additive which can be fed either as a meal sprinkled on the feed or in treacle form when it is mixed with warm water and used to dampen the feed.

Linseed is excellent for the coat and is often mixed in small amounts with boiled feed and fed two or three times a week. It should be soaked overnight, then boiled and simmered until the 'seeds' crack.

Boiled feed, fed two or three times a week, can consist of barley and/or oats with the linseed. It is excellent fed during the winter to fatten horses but is not generally fed during the competition season, except with a mash or if a horse tends to lose too much condition.

Boiled food is an excellent nutritious addition to the horse's diet, but should not be given once he is doing fast work (except as a mash). There are several ways of boiling the food: this photograph, for example, shows a metal bucket placed in a boiler; or the food can be put in a large saucepan in the oven

Salt should be fed daily in the feed and extra should be given in hot weather, along with electrolytes if the horse is working hard and likely to require them. This will be the case in hot climates where continuous dehydration may be taking place, or during an event. Electrolytes replace salts and essential body ions, etc, lost in sweat and evaporation.

Remember also that horses really enjoy carrots and your peelings will be much appreciated, as will those from apples. If feeding whole carrots and apples you should cut them up so that they cannot get caught in the horse's throat and cause choking.

How you feed your horse can make a great difference, especially with a fussy animal. It is extraordinary sometimes to see the same ingredients being given by one person and eaten up, yet exactly the same may be hardly touched when given by another.

Try and assess your horse's likes and dislikes. Does he like his feed wet, damp or dry? Try and mix the feed thoroughly so that it remains light. Add a little variety here and there. Remember to cut down if the horse has a day off or is unable to work. When the horse has just come back tired from competing do not give a big feed but a small nutritious one. It's likely he will be hungry the next day if fully recovered.

If the horse is not eating and there is no apparent reason it is often better to drop a feed; he may be getting worked up and excited about his career. Horses will usually eat better at night so it may be best to give a tea and supper feed rather than one at lunchtime. Some horses like to eat in mangers, others on the floor, but whatever they eat in be sure that it is kept clean. Nothing is likely to put a horse off quicker than the smell of sour food in a dirty feed bin. Water buckets also should be frequently sponged out.

Hay
Bulk food is essential to the horse's wellbeing and the ratio of bulk/ roughage to concentrates should rarely be less than 50:50, although with certain horses it could go as far as 40:60 when they are getting fit. Grass is nature's food of choice but the stabled horse requires the next best substitute in the form of hay. This must be of good quality, sweet smelling and non dusty. Hay comes in various different types but generally 'seed' hay is considered best for the competition horse and, if it has been well made, should have retained much of the goodness from the grass and be high in protein. Generally speaking, conventionally-made hay is considered at its best from six to eighteen months after it is made. If fed earlier it can still be rather 'rich' and can cause colic. Fed much later it starts to lose its nutritional value.

Hay, if not of top quality, can sometimes be a bit dusty, causing an allergy in the horse. Vacuum packed hay or horshage can solve the problem. It is most important that only the very best quality hay is used for competing horses.

One method of damping dust from a haynet. This, however, does little good to the hay itself, which should be soaked properly overnight in a dustbin or similar container, to allow the harmful spores in the hay to swell to their maximum size so they do not then enter the lungs

Well made soft hay can be very good so long as it is not dusty but it tends to have a lower protein content. It should be sweet- smelling and springy. Whatever hay is used it must be remembered that it will only be as good as the land from which it has come.

Some horses cough quite a lot with hay. If this cannot be controlled by damping the hay, or soaking it overnight and hanging it up in a net to drain before feeding, one of the 'horsehage' or vacuum packed hays can be tried. With this system the hay is produced and packed in sealed bags so that the moisture content is retained, and it tends to have a higher protein content. Smaller amounts should be fed. Once opened it must be consumed within four or five days and should be kept at a distance from normal hay or straw so that it retains its dust-free quality.

Hydroponics is a system whereby grass is produced in a machine, cut after a few days growth and fed immediately to the horse, thereby doing away with the dust problem altogether. It is worth looking into the costs and possible benefits of this system.

BEDDING

Bedding should be comfortable, protect the horse from injury and be warm in winter yet not get too heating in hot weather. The main types are straw, shavings and paper.

Straw
Straw is traditionally the bedding of choice, being warm, having good drainage qualities and being relatively cheap and easy to get in most areas. Wheat straw is the best but with modern harvesting methods removing the choke from barley effectively, barley straw is widely used. Oat straw should not be used.

Nothing looks nicer than a well prepared straw box. Problems are that if bad-quality straw is used it can be dusty, and horses sometimes like to eat it (whether it's good or bad straw!) and may cough.

Shavings
Shavings, if available, are springy, fairly good for drainage and fairly warm. Once down are moderately dust-free and easy to muck out. Problems are sometimes experienced in trying to get shavings, and when new they get everywhere when the horse lies down. If not kept dry they tend to cause foot problems, but these should be avoidable with good stable management.

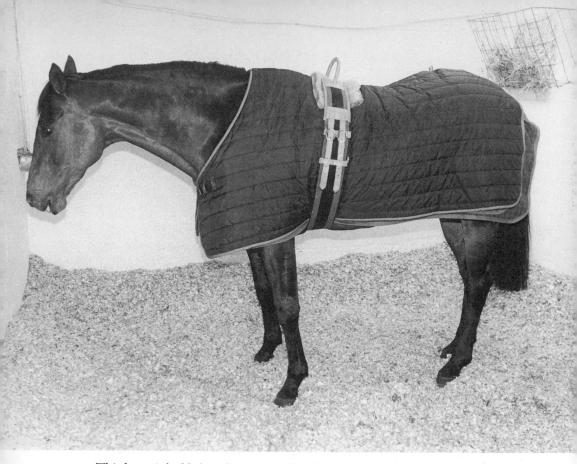

This horse is bedded on shavings, well banked up at the sides to prevent injury when rolling or lying down. Horses that tend to cough are generally better stabled on shavings or paper, and fed soaked hay or horshage, with well damped feed and plenty of fresh air. The hooped roller is to stop it rolling over and getting 'cast' in the stable. An anti-cast roller helps to prevent a horse getting cast, as it is supposed to prevent the animal rolling right over and getting stuck. Some horses, however, still manage to get cast, even when such precautions are taken

Paper

Paper has the big advantage of being dust-free and, if you are lucky, you can probably get together enough paper to be able to shred your own or find someone who will do this for you if you have just one or two horses. Produced commercially it is still fairly difficult to get and expensive. It is quite difficult to keep it tidy and muck out. However, it is undoubtedly of great value to the horse with breathing problems or who coughs.

There are several other types of bedding such as peat, bark and sawdust but you must choose whatever is suitable and easy to acquire paying particular attention to drainage and dust. Also consider how

34

easy it is to dispose of, storage, and whether you have got the right equipment to deal with it. A good sized wheelbarrow and tools make mucking out easy but poor tools can mean hours of extra time to do this basic chore. Always ensure that there is enough bedding to prevent the horse injuring itself when it gets down or rolls.

VENTILATION

In the United States most horses are stabled in the barn system, which is extremely convenient for everyone as everything is under one roof. Most barns are well ventilated and have plenty of height to allow a good circulation of air. This is extremely important and will make a great difference to the horse's wellbeing. Pokey little stables are not good and there are some conversions whereby cattle yards have been turned into barns which are very low and narrow. Unless great care is taken to ensure that there is adequate ventilation, problems can arise because a free flow of fresh air is not available. Any bugs in the atmosphere tend to hang around and a build-up of dust is inevitable.

A barnful of horses eagerly awaiting their tea. This system of stabling horses is becoming increasingly popular and is very easy to work in. Unless the horses can see out, however, it can lead to boredom with associated results. The spread of disease can also be a problem, so special precautions are necessary; but the system's drawbacks are definitely outweighed by the advantages

Always make sure your horses have good clean air running through their stables. If it is very hot arrange for extra ventilation such as fans to keep the horses cool.

SHOEING

Regular shoeing and good footcare are one of the most important aspects of good stable management. Feet should be picked out twice a day and inspected for loose clenches, and a regular shoeing routine must be adopted. Your farrier will advise you on any problems but do make a point of asking him for advice if the horse moves in a particular way, wears down its shoes excessively or is prone to knocks.

The angle of the foot and how it is shod can be of extreme importance, especially for the event horse who has to jump on such varied ground, uphill, over big drops, on the hard, the soft, rough ground etc, as well as doing hours of roadwork – especially in Britain – during the early fitness stage.

The things you must watch out for are that the shoe has been made to fit the horse and not the other way round. The toe should be reduced and the heels lowered as necessary, equally on both sides so that the horse stands squarely and evenly. Shoes should be of suitable weight for the type of work being done and must be securely and evenly nailed with the clenches well 'bedded'.

Always discuss studs and where you want them so that the farrier can make up the shoe with stud holes. In Britain it is more usual to have one hole on the outside nearer the heel and then the studs, which vary in size and shape, can be used according to the state of the ground. In the United States practices vary with the type of ground and often two studs are used, one on the inside and one on the outside. The aim should be to help the horse keep his footing in the best possible way with the minimum of interference.

CARE OF LEGS

The event horse has to cope with tough conditions and its legs have to take the strain of all this, so it is only right that the legs are given every possible care and attention. The golden rule with leg care is to react quickly to the slightest indication of a problem, however small. So many problems could have been prevented if they had been spotted and treated early enough. A few days rest at the right time can work wonders.

Care of the feet is a daily chore which is absolutely vital to the horse's soundness. Daily picking out and regular oiling will keep the feet in good condition. Foot problems are one of the most common causes of lameness. The shoe will have to be removed if an abscess or bruised foot causes unsoundness, so that effective hot tubbing and poulticing can commence

Shoeing and general foot care are very important, especially for the competition horse. During the season, shoeing every three to four weeks is vital to be certain that the horse will always be in good shape. Check your horse's movement regularly to see if any change in the way it is shod would be beneficial. If so, discuss the problem with your farrier and see if some slight adjustments might be helpful

Knowing your horse's legs has to be the first priority, caring for them the second. Get to know the feel of them, whether they are consistently cold, how they react before and after work, any slight hot spots and if these come and go or are a new reaction. Any lumps or bumps, soft swellings or hard ones, puffiness, and any changes to the normal must all be treated with great respect. The best time to get a proper idea is first thing in the morning and again in the evening. It is impossible to get a true picture if the horse has had bandages on, so if worn these should be removed and the legs inspected half an hour later.

I am personally against wrapping and bandaging unless it is absolutely essential, except for 24-48 hours after a serious workout. My reasoning for this is that a tough horse is needed and, if you keep the legs wrapped, it will feel and react to bumps and bruises much more. Left to its own devices it will toughen up that little bit more. This does not mean, however, that if the horse does need any sort of attention it will not get it!

Any bumps or bruises should immediately be treated with crushed ice for 24 hours to prevent further bruising. Watch out for knocks to joints. The fetlocks (ankles) are vulnerable and boots or bandages for protection of this joint are a wise precaution. Once you get an enlargement around the joint area it is difficult to get rid of, but it is always worth studying your horse's movement with the farrier to see if the shoes can be set under a little or a three-quarter shoe used to help stop a bruise. If bandages are used for work make sure that they come down over the joint far enough to protect that particular point of the leg.

In icy or slippery conditions it is a sensible precaution to ride with work kneepads just in case the horse goes down on the road. It is also quite a good idea to turn the fit horse out at first with some form of leg protection, as often they buck and kick around and can easily knock themselves.

Wounds should be thoroughly cleaned and treated with an antiseptic powder or spray. Always call the vet if there is any risk of infection or if the horse requires an injection. Tetanus must always be uppermost in one's mind. In America most stables carry a much more comprehensive medicine chest than those found in Britain and drugs are much more freely available over the counter for a wide variety of uses.

Never let a rub or any soreness go untreated, and change equipment such as boots or bandages if they are causing discomfort or chafing.

Keep the legs clean and free from sweat and dirt. Thoroughly wash them in pure soap after serious work to remove stale sweat etc, which can start to irritate if care is not taken. There are numerous leg washes designed to tone up skin and tissue and these are beneficial after work. Watch out for any skin rashes and keep a careful eye on heels, especially in wet weather. Soreness in this area can be very painful. The heels must be kept dry and warm. A little grease can be added if they show signs of chafing.

Turning out is very relaxing for the stabled horse and a little grass is always beneficial so long as the paddock is safe and well fenced, kept as worm-free as possible and has fresh water available. If two horses are to be turned out together and both are shod make sure that they know one another well and are unlikely to kick. The saying 'Two's company, three's none' can be very apt in this situation and it is usually wiser not to risk more out together unless the horses are being let down and shoes removed.

GROOMING

Good daily grooming is important for the wellbeing of the horse. It helps to keep the coat in proper condition and stimulates the circulation.

Sponging of the eyes, nose and dock is refreshing, especially in hot sticky weather, and all sweat round the ears, face, elbows etc should be carefully removed by hand rubbing if the horse is a bit sensitive.

The legs should be carefully inspected and all dirt removed, any little nicks or bruises treated, the feet picked out and hooves oiled. Always check the state of the shoes, tap down any risen clenches and call the farrier if attention is required.

Keep your grooming kit clean and always finish the horse off with a good dust over with a stable rubber to get that final gloss to his coat. A sharp pair of scissors can be used to keep him trimmed up and tidy. The mane and tail should be pulled as necessary and the tail bandaged daily to keep it in good shape. Never leave tail bandages on overnight in case they are too tight and interfere with the circulation.

GENERAL

'The eye of the master' is a great saying and at the end of the day, however well run your yard or careful you are, it is what you see that will tell you if all is well with your horse. Study him regularly and assess how he is progressing in fitness and condition.

Ask yourself if he is too thin or too fat, and if so be sure to adjust his food rations accordingly. Does he look well in himself, is he happy in his work, have you really done all the basics meticulously to prepare him in the best possible way? These questions should always be in your mind and any doubts acted upon straight away. Plan ahead and work out what is required for that particular horse so that you can do such things as worming, flu-vacs etc when the horse can have a few days easy afterwards, and not just when he ought to be having a cross-country school or gallop. It is these little details which will make all the difference in the end.

One thing which should be remembered, however, is that eventers are better off being on the lean side than too fat. This was well demonstrated at the World Championships in Kentucky in 1978 when the Argentinian horses arrived looking (to most people) very hollow and thin. In the extreme heat and humid conditions encountered there these horses completed the competition with few ill-effects, whilst my own and many others who supposedly 'looked' in better health succumbed to the very hot conditions, and took longer to recover.

CLIPPING

Clipping is done to allow the horse to work without getting unnecessarily hot. Some horses grow very thick coats, especially in winter, whilst others do not but the advantages of clipping are such that nearly every horse in serious work gets clipped at some stage.

Depending on the climate, horses generally are clipped out whenever it becomes obvious that they are at a disadvantage and likely to be hampered in their work.

There are various types of clip: the full clip, hunter clip, trace clip, blanket clip and variations of these. Personally I favour the hunter clip for the event horse, where the body is fully clipped out except for an optional saddle patch and the legs are left unclipped. Nature gave the animal its coat for warmth and protection and to me it seems a shame to remove the coat. However, if it is very hot and the horse is prone to sweating there may well be a case for taking everything off, especially during the summer months.

Blanket clips and trace clips are useful when the horse is starting work in a cold area, but once it really starts to be schooled the coat will have to come off.

If you are thinking of roughing the horse off after a certain competion, it is sensible to plan your clipping so that the horse can grow his coat as soon as possible but in very hot conditions the less coat the horse carries, the better.

Care must be taken that the clipped horse is not left in a draught as it can easily get chilled and the long back muscles get tight. Coolers, sweat rugs and towelling sheets are ideal to place over the clipped horse in hot weather. In cold weather the clipped horse should be regularly checked to ensure it is not getting cold, which will affect its condition as the horse will be using up its reserves of sugar and starch to keep warm rather than to produce energy.

Rugs

Nature gave horses a warm thick coat for the winter which is then shed for a finer summer one. Left in their natural state the build-up of grease in the coat meant that it also acted as a waterproof protection, but the stabled horse is usually clipped out and groomed thoroughly to keep it clean and free from grease and dirt.

The New Zealand rug enables the horse to be turned out in wet weather. Event horses benefit from a spell in the field every day if at all possible. When using a New Zealand rug for the first time give the horse time to get used to the straps between the legs and the rustle of the fabric before letting him loose outside. Never take risks by altering the rug in the field without a second person to hold the horse

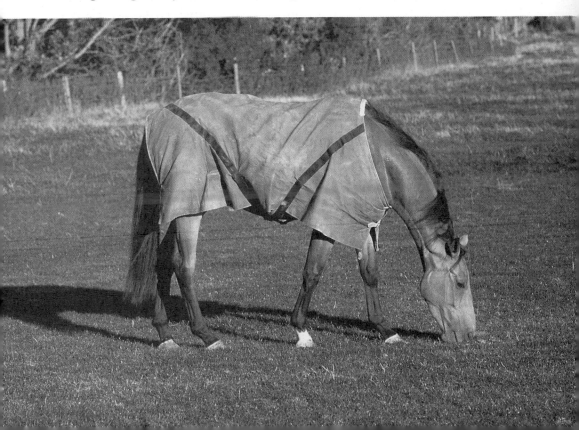

Tack rooms are perhaps the most important place in any yard. They need to be well organised, and kept clean and tidy so that everyone knows where equipment is kept. Safety is an important factor to be taken into consideration; all tack rooms should be locked and the key kept in a safe place when not in use or when no one is around

To compensate for this there are a vast number of rugs to choose from for every type of weather condition imaginable, varying from summer sheets to anti-sweat rugs, coolers, blankets, washable and unwashable stable rugs, New Zealand rugs of canvas, antislip rugs that do not require rollers etc. You name it and it's all there somewhere, ranging in price from the relatively cheap to the ludicrously expensive.

What rugs you choose is really a matter of personal preference but make sure they are the correct fit for your horse. This is particularly important with the modern rugs that are shaped over the shoulders and quarters. Watch carefully that your horse is not getting pressure sores on his neck or withers and be sure you have a good pad under the roller if used. Summer sheets and coolers are always useful, as are those made from towelling which are somehow warm and absorbent but not too hot. Sweat rugs are to be found in every stable and the choice of stable rugs and blankets depends on the weather conditions and climate. You need to be careful of some of the manmade materials which do not breathe adequately, leaving the horse to sweat underneath. In colder climates the New Zealand rug is ideal for turning the horse out. There are several on the market that have detachable linings to ensure that the horse will be warm enough whatever the weather.

Whatever you have in your stable try and keep it in good state of repair, as horses are notoriously destructive and it does not take long for them to break the fastenings, rip the sides, chew the fronts and generally get everything into a mess! If you cannot do it yourself a trip to the saddlers before the problem gets out of hand will be well worth while.

CHAPTER 3

Fitness and Basic Training

Not only does the event horse have to be very fit but he also has to be fit for three different disciplines. While one helps the other to a certain extent there is a lot of work involved in building the horse up to his peak, especially if you are aiming for a three-day event.

The emphasis must be on achieving a gradual build-up and, particularly with the horse that has been out for some time, it is vitally important that he is not put under pressure until his tendons, ligaments and muscles have tightened and hardened to maximum tone, so that they are not put under any strain during the first stage.

FIRST STAGE – SLOW WORK

While every nation has adopted slightly different techniques there is no question about the way to start getting the horse fit, and that is: slowly. Walking for the first two to four weeks is universal. In Britain we are relatively lucky to be able to ride on most roads fairly safely, especially in country areas, and this is the ideal place to start.

Walking for three-quarters of an hour during the first week on the road, building up to 1½ hours by the end of the second is the normal system. The flat smooth surface of the road does not strain anything and at walk is an excellent method of toning everything up.

If roadwork is not possible then working in a school or training field, or along good tracks, is the best alternative. The surface in a school may be fairly heavy so be careful not to overdo the horse; walking in deeper going can be very hard work. The aim in these conditions should be to do less for a little longer. Slow trotting in large circles and basic suppling exercises can be introduced after the first ten days, but only trot for short periods and do not ask the horse to work on the bit for too long at a time, particularly if he was totally unfit at the beginning.

For the horse that has only had a month or so off the process can be speeded up, but even so the first fortnight at walk only should not be dropped. These animals can be made to work a little harder on the bit but should not be overextended.

Long-reining a young horse is a useful way for getting him used to the hand aids, and for teaching him to go forward onto the bit. It is important when starting that the horse is not frightened by the two reins. This should only be done by a professional to start with, but is a very good method which used to be more fashionable than it is today

Trotting up hills is an excellent way of fittening horses, and it also teaches horses to balance themselves. This particular horse is not stretching forwards and swinging up the hill in trot, and the rider is getting slightly left behind

In this photograph the rider is working her horse in 'draw reins', or 'running reins' as they are sometimes called. Draw reins should only be used by the experienced rider; in the wrong hands they can do more harm than good. This rider has her draw reins fitted correctly, from the hand to the bit to the saddle. One often sees draw reins incorrectly fitted (from the bit to the girth in between the forelegs), which forces the horse's head down in quite a painful position

For those animals coming back into work after some sort of injury a much longer period of walking may have been advised by the vet. In this case you need to allow time to build up their walk programme gradually to up to 2 to 2½ hours daily. As they get fitter they may also start to get a bit playful and so it is necessary to add variety to their work by finding some good long hills to go up and down, provided they are not too steep, as well as practising simple suppling exercises and transitions from collected to extended walks, halts etc.

If you are lucky enough to have hills for fitness work you will find you need do far less later on when it comes to the galloping stage. Hill work really makes the muscles and the lungs work hard and increases their capacity towards maximum achievement.

There is no doubt that some people find this stage very monotonous and boring, and I have heard of all sorts of ways to relieve this situation. One girl told me she had done a Spanish language course with her Walkman in place, and another dictated letters into a dictaphone! I presume the 'clip-clops' made interesting background sounds to whoever had to decipher it all afterwards! A word of warning however if using such novel ideas – you will not be able to hear approaching traffic when wearing headphones, so always be alert and observant to your surroundings.

Once this first walking or slow period is done, increase the work by introducing more trotting and gradually decreasing the walking. It is best to do a slow trot keeping your horse on the bit. Far too many riders go out on roads and trot too fast. This only jars the legs and prevents the horse getting the full benefit of extending and contracting his working muscles in a steady rhythm, which is such an important part of the fitness procedure.

As the trot work progresses try to make sure you are continuing to build up the fitness programme week by week. Your aim is to be doing a little more, not necessarily timewise as you should not need to be out for more than 1½ to 2 hours maximum, but the type of work needs to be harder. It is the quality rather than the quantity that now needs emphasising.

Depending on the fitness of your horse when you started, this type of road work will probably need to last for two to four weeks. Those unable to do road work will be continuing to work horses indoors, gradually building on the quality of work but never straining the horse. Little and often is always best at this early stage.

SECOND STAGE – SCHOOLING

Once you have conscientiously carried out the slow build-up to tone and harden muscles and tendons in the first stage of fitness, you can then move on to the stretching, suppling and schooling stage safe with the knowledge that the horse has been well prepared to cope with the extra work this demands.

While you need to continue with some hacking out if possible you must now, again gradually, start to ask the horse to settle down and do some more demanding work on the flat. Always start with a period of walking to allow the horse to stretch and loosen up well, especially if you have to do this in a school. Then ask the horse to come together and take the contact, building up to a series of loops and circles on both reins. As he settles into his work, introduce transitions from one pace to another and ask for greater obedience by collecting and extending. Initially, avoid doing too much without a break. It is better to do a series of short sessions rather than overstrain by doing a longer time. If the

This is a lovely picture of a horse being allowed freedom to relax and stretch whilst the rider softens seat and hands in the middle of a training session. The horse will need breaks in between work so that muscles can be rested. It is much better to build up work gradually than to overdo training sessions by too much work all in one go

horse starts to get heavy in the hand this may well mean his neck muscles are aching and so it is much better to give him 3 or 4 minutes walking on a long rein than to continue. A horse may also do this if his work is boring or repetitive and the rider is not pushing him up into the bridle with a strong enough leg.

EXERCISES

Circles

Once the horse is working well in all paces you must think of the movements to be performed in your dressage tests. At novice level this will consist of 20m circles in both trot and canter, so these must be worked on in order that you achieve a smooth and consistent circle maintaining an even rhythm throughout.

The most important thing is suppling your horse first by frequent changes of rein and being sure to ride him through the corners with the correct bend. This will only be achieved if you keep your inside leg forward on the girth with a strong feel whilst your outside leg is placed

further back to control the quarters. Your inside hand will then guide the horse and the outside one control the degree of bend, which should not be more than that required to follow the line you are taking.

Serpentines and Loops

Serpentines may be required in some tests. What is required here is for the judge to be able to see the change of bend across the centre line whilst the horse maintains a consistent even pace. Start by doing three loops. If you have a full sized arena to work in this will consist of three 20m half-circles. The horse should straighten for a couple of strides over the centre line and you should aim for a smooth change of bend.

In a small arena the angles will be more acute and the turns smaller to fit into the 40m length. The turns across the arena will in effect be diagonally across, so more attention to the change of bend must be practised as well as being sure that you achieve loops of consistently even size. When schooling you can practise doing more loops if the horse is sufficiently balanced and can maintain a good rhythm.

Loops off and then back onto the track, usually of 5m, again require an even rhythm and a smooth supple bend off the track. During this exercise the judges will want to see that the horse bends through his body with no resistance or stiffness.

It can be helpful to practise working round a barrel or similar object placed halfway down the school at about 4m off the track to get an idea of the degree of curve required, but be very careful that you do not restrict the horse with too tight an inside rein as you return to the track. Allow the outside hand to be the guiding one until you return to the track, when the inside one will take over to go round the corner.

Horse and rider working on the flat at home, practising their 10-metre circles in canter. The rider is looking around the shape of his circle, and his shoulder is following the movement of the horse's outside shoulder. His seat is central with a strong, secure leg, pushing the horse into the bridle. The horse shows correct bend and is well balanced between hand and leg. Notice just how far underneath the horse the inside leg has to come, especially on the smaller circles, which requires a great deal of impulsion

This rider is schooling on the flat at home. Her horse is wearing brushing boots in front and fetlock boots behind. These will protect the horse from any knocks he may get during training. She is riding in 15-metre circles, and the horse is following the line of the circle nicely and is showing correct bend of his body. The rider is in a good, effective position, with a soft hand, deep seat and a strong secure leg. She is looking around the shape of her circle and is following with her shoulder

The Half Halt

One of the most important exercises used when training the horse is the half halt. This will not be specifically asked for in a test but is used throughout the horse's training and can perhaps be best described as a rebalancing or pre-preparation for any movement.

The legs should be applied fairly strongly just before the rider uses a restraining hand and sits deeper in the saddle. This will result in a shortened frame of the horse as his legs come more underneath his body, and more active steps ready for the next instruction. It is important that the rider makes the most of this and does not then release the extra energy too quickly, but just eases the reins slightly into whatever is required. If the horse resists or does not respond enough to the rider's aids, a stronger leg and deeper seat plus giving and taking with the hands should achieve a result. Practice makes perfect and the horse must be taught to respond to this most useful and important exercise.

The Halt

If the half halt has been perfected than the halt is the obvious progression.

In preparation for the halt the rider will first ask for a couple of half halts, then halt with stronger aids but immediately give with the reins a little so that the horse can stand still evenly balanced and square on all four legs. It should remain absolutely still and this will take time and practice. If the horse does not halt square then he must always be pushed forward and never pulled back into a halt. This will always be severely penalised.

When practising at home it is best to push the horse forwards and try again. Remember to relax so that the horse remains calm and reward him when he halts well. The rider should be able to feel if the halt is not square as the horse will be dipped towards the leg that is left behind. If the rider puts his leg behind the girth lightly on that side the horse will then bring that leg forward, but do not be too strong or he may bring it too far or, worse, move away so that he becomes crooked.

Remember to practise your salute so that the horse is accustomed to this before you try it out in front of the judges. Ladies take both reins into the left hand, the right hand is placed straight down by the rider's side, she lowers her head in salute and then quietly takes up the reins again. Gentlemen take off their hats and place them at their sides. If a harness is worn gentlemen do the same as the ladies. Keep it smooth and unhurried; it is an important part of your test so it needs to look good. First impressions are very important, so it is well worth getting this absolutely right; your entry tells the judge a great deal about the obedience and training of the horse. A beaming smile just might earn you an extra point for general impression – it's worth a try!

The Rein Back

The well schooled horse should rein back willingly. This can first be taught from the ground or with the rider on top. If teaching from the ground the rider should take the reins and lightly ease the horse back a step by tapping him on the forearm or fetlock, saying 'Back' with each step. It is important to tap the near and then off fore in sequence so that the horse learns to go back to command. It is best to do just a couple of steps back and then have a break before repeating until the horse fully understands what is being asked of him.

If reining back with the rider on top then it is best to have a helper to start with, again to just tap the legs back in sequence with the rider

This rider is asking the horse to rein back. The rein back is a two-time movement in which the horse moves back in diagonal pairs. The rider has lightened his seat, and is closing his legs around the horse into a soft but restricting hand

using his voice. The rider should have his legs on the horse and restrict forward movement with the hand. As the horse realises he cannot go forward he will step back. As the horse steps backwards the rider will start to use alternate aids to keep the horse straight as he picks up first one then the other diagonal pairs for legs. As the movement becomes established the horse should lower his hindquarters as they become more engaged. The rein back is an excellent movement for helping collection and balance.

Counter-Canter

Loops off the track form the start of counter-canter and these are gradually increased in size as confidence is gained. The secret here is to keep the balance consistently on the one rein regardless of the change in direction.

Be careful not to shift your weight suddenly and thus force the horse off balance so that he changes leg. Keep the size of your loop even and not too deep until you feel your horse has learnt how to cope and what is expected of him. Make sure he starts in a shortish canter, so work on a few transitions from working to medium and back again, pushing him well up into the restraining hand until he feels sufficiently balanced and off his forehand to find the movement easy to achieve. Ultimately it should be possible to do a complete circle in counter-canter and this is a particularly useful exercise to help the horse improve his balance, supple his back and ribs and bring his hocks more underneath him.

Transitions

The smoothness of transitions from one pace to another is one of the key issues when it comes to the judge assessing your test, so these need to be perfected as early as possible. How they are performed will depend on the standard of schooling so far achieved by your horse.

The young and relatively unschooled horse will not be capable of responding immediately so the rider must give and retake the reins to slow him down, using the legs and trying the basics of the half halt whilst also saying 'Whoa' to the horse. Keep the hands low and, when the horse has come down to trot, give him time to establish a rhythm. Practice makes perfect and repeated efforts will help the horse to understand,. However, if things are not going too well it is often best to do something else and then come back to the exercise. Trotting to canter and back to trot is often best done on a large circle changing the rein frequently.

Having just lengthened this horse's stride across the diagonal of the arena, the rider is about to ask the horse to 'come back' to a working trot. She will do this by closing her legs softly around the horse, and pushing into a soft but slightly restraining hand. The photograph shows clearly the period of suspension in the trot, when all four feet are off the ground

The more schooled horse will be better balanced, able to cope with half halts and lighter on the forehand, and should be able to perform transitions both up and down from canter, trot and walk to halt.

Remember that whatever the pace, all transitions whether upward or downward, must be ridden forwards – it is one of the most important aspects of all riding. Think forwards.

Lateral Work

Lateral movements are useful to supple the horse, particularly his quarters, and to achieve greater balance and freedom of the shoulder. To do any of the exercises properly the horse must move energetically forwards and sideways on two tracks. The bend depends slightly on the degree of training and the engagement of the hocks. The shoulder-in, travers, renvers and half pass are the four basic movements.

The degree of bend is the important factor. This should be almost even from head to tail. Too often riders make the mistake of having too much bend in the neck resulting in the horse falling out over the outside shoulder. Lateral work should only be ridden for short periods of time and is mainly done from collected trot. The rider should have more weight on the inside seat bone pushing down into the inside heel. He must keep his shoulders parallel to the horse's shoulders and his hips parallel to the horse's hips. His hands must remain on each side of the horse's withers.

In shoulder-in the forehand is brought slightly in off the track, so that the horse is on three tracks with the outside foreleg being directly in front of the inside hind leg. The horse is bent slightly away from the direction in which he is going. The rider's inside leg is placed close to the girth and pushes the horse forwards and creates the lateral bend in the ribs, whilst the outside leg placed a little further back controls the hindquarters and stops the horse swinging off the track. The outside rein controls the degree of bend in the neck and the inside one keeps the horse bent to the inside.

The object of shoulder–in is to create lightness, a higher degree of collection and balance, and ultimately to improve straightness. To start with it is best to do a 5m circle to start the lateral bend, or to come from the corner. It should end before the next corner when the rider should realign the horse's forehand back with the quarters and continue to ride him forwards in rhythm.

Watch out for the common fault of using too strong an inside rein, resulting in the horse falling out onto the outside shoulder. This can be corrected by controlling the bend with the outside hand and pushing the horse more forward. Unevenness can be another fault and this may be corrected by first re-establishing a good rhythm and balance before asking again for a few shoulder–in steps.

In travers the horse's quarters are brought in off the track so that the outside hind leg is a little to the inside of the inside front. The lateral bend is controlled by the inside leg. To finish the movement the forehand is aligned with the quarters and the horse is then brought sideways back to the track and ridden straight forwards.

In renvers the horse's forehand moves on a track half a step inside the track of the inside hind foot but is bent towards the direction in which he is travelling. The horse will only be able to maintain his balance in renvers if the rider sits correctly with his weight on the inside seatbone, with his shoulders parallel to the horse's and his hips parallel to the horse's quarters.

The most common faults in both travers and renvers are too much bend in the neck and too much angle, resulting in loss of rhythm and balance. In either case the horse should be ridden forwards and the bend in the neck corrected. These are excellent suppling exercises and are normally performed in collected trot.

Leg yielding is the first step towards the half pass. The horse is asked to travel sideways, bent slightly away from the direction in which he is travelling. It is normally ridden in a working trot but is best started in walk. It can also be done in canter.

The movement starts with a half halt and then the rider asks the horse to go sideways with a strong inside leg. It is not that easy to keep the horse moving sideways but the rider must adapt his hands and legs continuously to keep the horse going in the direction asked.

This exercise is requested in several of the American tests but not in the English ones. It is good for suppling and to start lateral exercises but some people find it confusing to do leg yielding, which has the bend going away from the direction of travel, and then have to get used to half pass in which the horse is bent towards the direction of travel. If you do find this difficult (as I did!) get your trainer to explain thoroughly what is required for the one exercise and perfect this before attempting the next.

The half pass is the most spectacular of the lateral movements. The horse moves forwards and sideways, looking in the direction towards which he is travelling. The horse is curved around the rider's inside leg as he travels diagonally across the arena. It is excellent for suppling horses on both sides. In eventing the half pass is only expected in trot but it can also be done in collected canter.

It is important to start with a half halt and correct bend. Then put the outside leg on behind the girth to push the horse over whilst the inside leg maintains the bend, being placed firmly on the girth. The horse must be kept moving forwards and sideways and not be allowed to lose any forward impulsion. Sometimes the horse will go too acutely sideways instead, so make sure that you are ready to push him forwards with both legs to correct if necessary. The half pass takes time to perfect so do not be too ambitious at first. It is better to get a few good strides and then drive the horse forwards before asking for some more. The half pass is used primarily to supple the horse and collect it, and should only be done from a collected pace.

The above exercises cover most of those required in eventing dressage tests and form the basis of all correct flat work. These should be practised and perfected gradually, using arenas both large and small where possible and aiming for attainable goals as time goes on and the horse becomes more experienced.

The two sizes of arena (20m × 40m and 20m × 60m) are used internationally for all dressage tests. The larger one is used for all FEI tests, and is favoured in most countries. In Britain, however, novice and intermediate tests are generally performed in the smaller arena to enable a greater number of horses to take part. The tests must be ridden from memory, with the judge awarding marks from 0 to 10 for each movement. For horse trials FEI tests there are generally three judges who sit at C and on the edge of the arena by H and M. For other tests and those ridden in the small arena the judges (either one or two) sit at C.

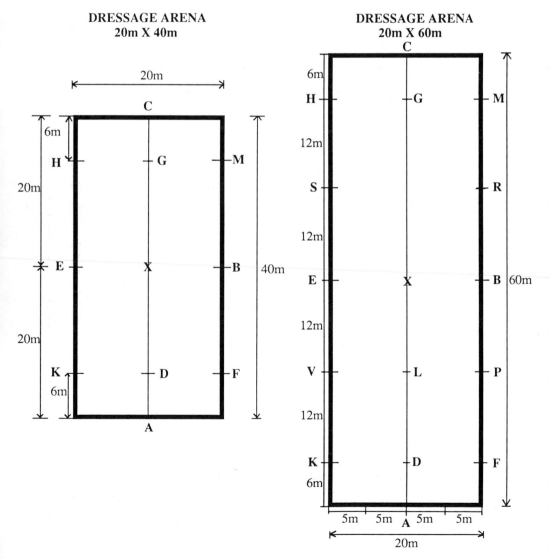

THE F.E.I
CONTINENTAL JUNIORS CHAMPIONSHIP
THREE-DAY EVENT
DRESSAGE TEST (1976)
Approximate Time - 8 mins

To be ridden in a snaffle or double bridle.
Spurs are compulsory   Max marks

1.	A	Enter at working canter	
	X	Halt-Immobility-Salute	
		Proceed at working trot	10
2.	C	Track to the left	
	EBE	Circle left 20m diameter	
	EA	Continue at working trot	10
3.	A	Down centre line	
	L	Circle left, 10m diameter	10
4.	LH	Medium trot	
	H	Working trot	10
5.	C	Halt-Rein back 4 steps-Proceed at working trot without halting	10
6.	BEB	Circle to right 20m diameter	
	BA	Continue at working trot	10
7.	A	Down centre line	
	L	Circle right 10m diameter	10
8.	LM	Medium trot	
	M	Working trot	10
9.	C	Halt-Immobility 4 seconds	
		Proceed at working trot	10
10.	HXF	Change rein at medium trot (rising)	
	F	Working trot	10
11.	KXM	Change rein at medium trot	
	M	Working trot	10
12.	C	Medium walk	
	HSXPF	Change rein at extended walk	
	F	Medium walk	10
13.	A	Working canter - circle right 20m diameter	10
14.	AC	Serpentine 3 loops, first and third true canter, second counter-canter	10
15.	MXK	Change rein at medium canter	
	K	Working trot	10
16.	A	Working canter - circle left 20m diameter	10
17.	AC	Serpentine 3 loops, first and third true canter second counter canter	10
18.	HXF	Change rein at medium canter	
	F	Working trot	10
19.	A	Down centre line	
	L	Working canter to the right	10
20.	G	Halt - Immobility - Salute	10
	A	Leave arena at walk on a long rein	

Collective marks:

1.	Paces (freedom and regularity)	10
2.	Impulsion (desire to move forward, elasticity of the steps and engagement of the hindquarters)	10
3.	Submission (attention and obedience, lightness and ease of movements, acceptance of the bridle)	10
4.	Position, seat of the rider, correct use of the aids	10

Arena 20m x 40m   TOTAL 240

N.B. In Horse Trials Advanced & FEI Tests all trot work is executed "sitting" unless otherwise indicated in the test concerned.

THE FEI YOUNG RIDERS
THREE DAY EVENT DRESSAGE TEST (1986)
Approximate Time - 7 mins 30 secs

To be ridden in a snaffle or double bridle

Spurs are compulsory   Max Marks

1.	A	Enter at working canter	
	X	Halt - Immobility - Salute	
		Proceed at working trot	10
2.	C	Track to the left	
	EBE	Circle to the left 20m diameter	10
3.	V	Half-circle of 10m diameter	
	LS	Half-pass (left)	10
4.	C	Halt - Rein back 5 steps	
		Proceed at working trot	10
5.	BEB	Circle to the right 20m diameter	10
6.	P	Half-circle of 10m diameter	
	LR	Half-pass (right)	10
7.	C	Halt - Immobility 5 seconds - Proceed at working trot	10
8.	HXF	Change rein at medium trot	
	F	Working trot	10
9.	KXM	Change rein at extended trot	
	M	Working trot	10
10.	C	Medium walk	
	HSXPF	Change rein at extended walk	
	F	Medium walk	10
11.	A	Circle at working trot 10m diameter	10
12.	A	Working canter - circle to the right 10m diameter	10
13.	AC	Serpentine 3 loops, the first and the third true canter the second counter-canter	10
14.	MXK	Change rein at medium canter	
	K	Working trot	10
15.	A	Circle at working trot 10m diameter	10
16.	A	Working canter - circle to the left 10m diameter	10
17.	AC	Serpentine 3 loops, the first and the third true canter, the second counter canter	10
18.	HXF	Change rein at medium canter	
	F	Working trot	10
19.	A	Down centre line	10
20.	G	Halt - Immobility - Salute	10
		Leave arena at a walk on a long rein at A	

Collective Marks:

1.	Paces (freedom and regularity)	10
2.	Impulsion (desire to move forward, elasticity of the steps and engagement of the hindquarters)	10
3.	Submission (attention and obedience, lightness and ease of movements, acceptance of the bridle)	10
4.	Position, seat the of rider, correct use of the aids	10

Arena 20m x 60m   TOTAL 240

NB. In Horse Trials Advanced and FEI Tests all trot work is executed "sitting" unless otherwise indicated in the test concerned.

THE F.E.I.
THREE-DAY EVENT DRESSAGE TEST - SENIOR (1990)

No.	Point	Movement	Marks
1.	A	Enter at working canter	
	I	Halt - Immobility - Salute	
		Proceed at working trot	10
2.	C	Track to the right	
	MRXVK	Medium trot (rising or sitting)	
	KA	Working trot	10
3.	A	Continue working trot	
		From corner: shoulder-in (left)	
	BXB	Circle to the left 10m diameter	10
4.	BG	Half-pass (left)	
	GCH	Working trot	10
5.	HXF	Change rein at extended trot	
	FA	Working trot	10
6.	A	Halt - rein back 4 to 6 steps - Halt	
		Proceed at working trot	10
7.	A	Continue working trot	
		From corner: shoulder-in (right)	
	EXE	Circle to the right 10m diameter	10
8.	EG	Half-pass (right)	
	GCM	Working trot	10
9.	MXK	Change rein at extended trot	
	KA	Working trot	10
10.	AF	Medium walk	
	FS	Change rein at extended walk	
	SH	Medium walk	10
11.	HCR	Working canter	10
12.	RBEBP	Medium canter (BEB: circle 20m diameter)	
	PF	Working canter	10
13.	FDB	Working canter (FD: half circle 10m diameter)	
	BRMCH	Counter canter	10
14.	HXF	Change rein at extended canter	
	FA	Working canter	10
15.	AK	Medium walk	
	KR	Change rein at extended walk	
	RM	Medium walk	10
16.	MCS	Working canter	10
17.	SEBEV	Medium canter (EBE: circle 20m diameter)	
	VK	Working canter	10
18.	KDE	Working canter (KD: half circle 10m diameter)	
	ESHCM	Counter canter	10
19.	MXK	Change rein at extended canter	
	KAL	Working canter	10
20.	LG	Working trot	
	G	Halt - Immobility - Salute	10
		Leave arena at a walk on a long rein at A.	

Collective Marks:

No.		Marks
1.	Paces (freedom and regularity)	10
2.	Impulsion (desire to move forward, elasticity of the steps and engagement of the hind quarters)	10
3.	Submission (attention and obedience, lightness and ease of the movements, acceptance of the bridle)	10
4.	Position and seat of the rider, correct use of the aids	10

Arena 20m x 60m   TOTAL 240

NB. The working, medium and extended trots, must be executed "sitting" unless the term "rising" is used in the test.

While this schooling on the flat is taking place – and this should continue throughout – it is important that the event horse's fitness programme is systematically continued. When the second stage of flat work and jumping training (which will be dealt with in the next chapter) is underway, it is time to think about the third and final stage of fitness. This is the lead-up period to the first event, the sharpening-up and final conditioning period.

THE THIRD STAGE

The condition of the horse should by now be such that he is fit and able to cope with quite a lot, having been in work for something between eight and twelve weeks. If you have built up the fitness properly all your horse now needs are a few gallops to clear his wind and some outings to give him a chance to get his eye in (and yours!) for what you are wanting him to do.

Fast Work
How much fast work your horse needs varies so much from horse to horse that it is difficult to generalise, but the thoroughbred or that type will usually need less than the halfbred or warmblood horse. Slow cantering helps to build up the lung capacity and should be done two to three times weekly for periods of up to 20–30 minutes, with walks of up to 5 minutes twice in between. Remember everything must be a gradual build-up, so with your first canter you will perhaps canter slowly for 5–10 minutes which can then be increased to 12–15 minutes after four or five sessions if the horse feels ready. Remember that the lazy horse will need pushing a bit to make him work hard enough to build up fitness, whilst the tireless sort needs to be kept quiet so that it does not 'peak' too soon. Short faster bursts once or twice a week varying from ½ to ¾ mile will clear the wind near to a competition.

Try to keep to a routine and plan back from your competitions to decide when you are going to 'work' your horse. Generally a work day needs to be followed by a rest day then two to three days 'normal' before another work day or competition. Sit down with your trainer

---

These two riders are just starting off on a hack: an important part of the horse's basic fitness routine. These two horses are well protected against any knocks or bangs which might occur, and are wearing brushing boots in front and fetlock boots behind. The riders are correctly turned out wearing hard hats, gloves and hard boots with heels. Notice too how happy and relaxed the four of them appear

and work out a plan to take you through this important third stage. It is important that it is a build-up stage, not one in which the horse is overworked and finished off before he ever gets to the competiton. All too often this happens when people panic, thinking their horses are not fit enough.

It is much the best plan to take your horse to his first event and ride him sensibly round to give him a nice outing and assess his fitness, and then go faster next time when he will have benefitted from his first experience.

Remember that cross-country schools and small competitions count as work days so it will not be necessary to fit in other gallops on those weeks. Try and do a few dressage or show jumping competitions in this third stage to get experience and get into the swing of things, whether building up to your very first horse trial or just the first of the season.

Interval Training

Many people, particularly in America, use this system to get their horses fit and it is important that a programme is devised to suit each horse once its basic fitness is achieved. In principle this method asks the horse to work then brings it back to rest but, before it has fully recovered, asks it to work again. A rest is again followed by fast work before the horse's heart rate has fully returned to normal. In this way the horse builds up endurance but it must never be overstressed.

The speed is vital to success, as are the lengths of the rest periods. Always work your horse on good ground, keep him well between hand and leg and never push him beyond his limits. Use hills wherever possible as these are excellent to fitten and supple the horse, and work up hills is worth twice the distance on the flat.

OTHER METHODS

The traditional method of getting horses fit through gradually doing a little more week by week and letting the horse 'tell' you when he is fit is well known, but it needs an experienced eye to assess this and to know when a little more or a little less is necessary for specific competitions. As far as fast work is concerned the saying 'If in doubt – don't' is quite sensible so long as you have carried out the slow work conscientiously. It is the way you ride a course, rather than the speed, which makes the difference between a good and a bad round. This will be discussed later in the chapter on competing.

Lengthening the stride is an important part of basic training on the flat. This rider has achieved excellent lengthening, and is driving the horse on well, but is losing some of the effect of his driving aids by leaning forward a little too much. It is most important to sit up well, and use your seat and legs to push the horse forward.

This rider is performing a very good shoulder-in, with the horse curved around the rider's inside leg and looking away from the direction in which he is travelling. The horse should be on three tracks for this movement, which can be seen clearly in this photograph. This exercise helps to supple the horse, and is widely used in all basic training. The rider must allow her shoulders to follow the angle of the horse's shoulders, and her hips should stay square in the saddle, in line with the horse's quarters

Swimming

Some horses get quite jarred by hard ground and as fast work would be inadvisable in this case, it is possible to build up their lung capacity in an equine pool. It is important to remember that this should only be used on a horse which is basically fit, whose legs are hard and who has done the early work. It is an excellent way to keep a horse going but care must be taken not to overdo him, especially until he is used to it. The same message of 'gradual build-up' applies.

The horse works extremely hard in the pool, both with his muscles and breathing, and it is better to put him in for a few minutes and bring him out again a couple of times than to overdo it by swimming him all in one go.

Swimming can be a very useful substitute for some horses in their fitness programme but before embarking on this treatment discuss carefully with your vet what distance and time the horse should start on and aim for.

When doing fast work be sure that your horse is adequately protected with boots or bandages at all times, as a knock at this stage could put you out and wreck your programme by weeks. Remember to keep everything in good condition and ready for use so that your horse is ready for his first big competition fit, sound and ready to compete.

The use of grids is an invaluable way of schooling the horse to cope with different fences. The simple grid shown here is encouraging the horse to stretch and 'round' over his fences. Make sure that the grids are built up gradually, and do not confront your horse with a confusing array of poles too early; this can put a young horse back in his training

Teaching the young horse how to jump different types of fences is essential if he is to build up confidence and perfect his technique over this type of obstacle. Once the horse has learnt how to jump neatly over a small drop fence, larger ones should prove little problem. This young horse looks happy and confident, and should be able to jump the bigger fence on the left easily, having worked out how to cope with the smaller obstacle first

CHAPTER 4

Jumping

Careful training over fences will ensure that your horse is fully prepared to cope with the demands of the sport. While the majority of horses have a more than adequate natural ability to jump the size of fence met eventing – and even at advanced level these do not exceed 3ft 11in – it is the technique that is so important. The rider, however, plays a very big part in all this and it's no good getting in a panic about the judges – you've got to 'think positive' and have a go from the start if you are going to be successful. I've seen some fairly strange reactions from riders who think they want to event, but will not commit themselves when it comes to the jumping, even when the fences are small. A positive mental attitude is perhaps priority number one before attempting anything serious with the horse, so find out what makes the rider tick. A stiff drink, strong words or whatever – it is vital that the rider is totally committed before the horse is asked to do anything.

Schooling on the flat, as discussed in the previous chapter, will enable the horse to be supple enough to turn into his fences with the right amount of impulsion, to increase or decrease the stride, and to approach with the right amount of collection and 'bounce'.

The next aspect is ensuring that the horse uses himself to the best of his ability over the fence, and is confident and willing. To achieve this he must be taught to approach, take off, land and rebalance himself to the very best of his ability. Obedience is one of the main factors, and the horse must learn to 'listen' to its rider and respond accordingly. This in turn builds up the confidence between horse and rider which is so important in creating a partnership to tackle fences of all the different types found in both show jumping and cross-country.

BASIC TRAINING (TROTTING POLES)

Regardless of the standard of your horse there is no better way of suppling and settling him than to trot him over poles. These should be set at a distance to suit your horse's stride but it will be in the region of

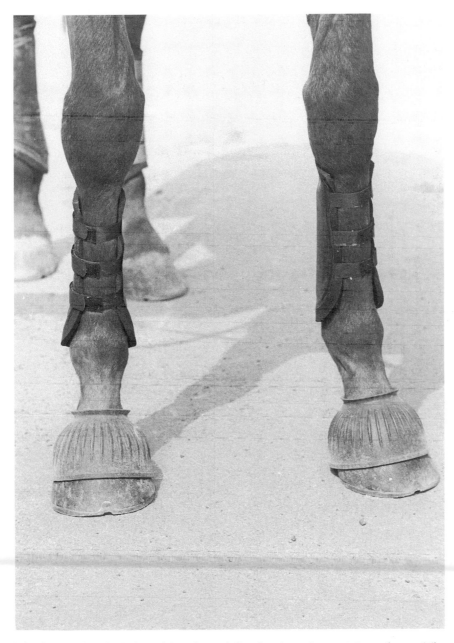

The horse's legs here have been dressed for showjumping practice at home. The open-fronted tendon boots on the front legs protect the vulnerable tendons, but allow a horse to 'feel' a fence if he hits it, by not covering the cannon bones. The horse must respect fences, and will not do so if over-protected. He is wearing over-reach boots and brushing boots behind

Raised poles will increase the effort required of the horse, and are the next obstacles to tackle after poles on the ground. It is a good way of increasing suppleness and co-ordination, and will help the horse to build up muscle and strength. It should not be over-used until the horse is sufficiently fit

1.25–1.30m (4ft–4ft 6in). The horse has to use himself well by picking up his legs as well as shoulders and quarters to do this exercise, and has to concentrate so as not to make a mistake. It is a good idea to walk quietly over the poles first and then, once the animal has relaxed, to progress to trot. The horse must be kept balanced and controlled and not allowed to rush at any time.

If you have some cavaletti the horse can be made to work even harder by having to lift his legs higher over these raised poles. Place your poles so that you can do a few together, then have a break and then do some more, to keep the horse concentrating. Make sure you change the rein and direction of approach and do not overdo the exercise.

Some horses rush badly, either through fear or overexcitement, and these must be trotted quietly in a circle over one or two poles only until they relax and settle into their work. Then you can gradually introduce more poles. It may be helpful to go back to walk and to twist and turn them through and over the poles before asking for the exercise again in trot.

Getting the horse used to poles on the ground encourages him to look down and this is important if the horse is going to jump over his fences with good style.

JUMPING SIMPLE FENCES

The young horse normally starts over small, simple fences quite early in its career, and should be popping over a variety of different types confidently and happily before being expected to jump anything too big or to attempt grids.

The older horse must be able to jump single fences quietly and without rushing. Very often these horses have learnt to rush at their fences and if this is the case a lot of time and patience is required to get them to trot and then canter quietly over fences. Jumping off a circle is good; sometimes the horse can be circled away from the fence, and sometimes jumped so that he is not sure what the rider has in mind and gradually will start to settle and 'listen'.

This rider's horse tends to rush at his fences, and to conquer this problem she is circling him around and through trotting poles. Once the horse has settled he will be asked to jump again. Her trainer is looking on and offering help and advice. Not only is it helpful to have someone on the ground to help with your riding and to manoeuvre poles and jumps, but it is also wise to have someone around in case you have a fall

GRIDS

The next stage is to introduce your horse to grids in order to increase his gymnastic ability and improve his alertness. Having done poles and single fences, it will not be difficult to accept a jump and then build up to a full line of a grid.

Cross-poles are better than a straight rail as the cross encourages the horse to 'pick up' neatly in front, and the angle of the cross-pole can be increased as the grid gets higher or harder. Gradually increase the grid by adding a pole on the ground and then another fence; this could be a straight rail, then perhaps another pole on the ground. Another cross-rail follows after a couple of jumps down the grid. This could then be made more interesting by the addition of a 'bounce'.

To do this keep the second element the same height as the first and place them approximately 3m (10ft) apart. Practise a couple of times so that the horse learns to shorten his stride to jump this easily and with confidence. Another pole on the ground and then a small spread could complete your grid. This will have helped to teach your horse to be

This horse is jumping an inviting cross pole, which has trotting poles in front to help him arrive at the fence at the correct pace and place. The rider is in basically good position, but is not really giving the horse enough freedom of his head and neck. Both horse and rider are correctly turned out for jumping

The cross pole is the most useful of training fences. It encourages the horse to jump the centre of the fence, and helps it to be neat in front. As the horse progresses in its training it is possible to increase its athletic ability by accentuating the height of the poles

neat in front (cross-poles), to shorten his stride (bounce), and to stretch over the fence (spread).

The grid you have built will in effect look something like this: pole – cross – pole – straight fence – straight fence – pole – spread. Add a pole at the end to encourage him to look down on landing. The distances from the poles on the ground to the fence will need to be approximately 3m (9–10ft) but you will be able to judge whether your horse has a longer or shorter stride by watching him over the poles on the ground first. It is very important to build up your grid gradually and not immediately confront your horse with a line of confusing fences. Have a helper to put up the fences when you decide to have a grid session and always end on a good note.

If you have a problem, go back a stage by taking away an element to build up confidence again. You may be asking too much. If the horse is overconfident and starts to rush you may need to increase the difficulty by making the fences a little higher, with the cross-poles in particular being raised. Change the grid regularly, depending on what lesson you want your horse to learn – there are numerous variations

This small grid is being jumped very neatly in front by this horse, who is looking ahead and concentrating hard. He does, however, need to lower his head more when jumping in order to raise his withers, and therefore use himself to the best of his ability

and it is best to design grids or gymnastics with your trainer, who knows you and your horse and can see straight away what is required to improve his technique and way of jumping.

Grids should only be done once the horse has mastered the art of jumping simple, straightforward fences, and should not be attempted until the young horse is physically strong and mature enough to cope with this fairly demanding work. They should only be of a height suitable for that particular horse's stage of training, and are particularly useful for the event horse who has to learn to cope with a tremendous variation in fences and strides as he works his way through the different levels of the sport.

COLOURED FENCES

Show jumps come in a variety of colours and shapes and it is important that your horse is not put off or caught out because he has not seen enough of these coloured fences, so do make a point of jumping the young or spooky type of horse over as many different fences as possible. Zig–zag shapes, large dots and so on can look quite daunting, especially if highly coloured with deep contrasts.

The different types of fences must also be jumped so that the horse is quite confident about tackling walls with and without gaps, gates, planks, spread fences with brush underneath, combinations of doubles and trebles, triples and verticals, etc. As you get more advanced, don't be caught out by water. The horse may have to jump this at certain levels in show jumping and at advanced eventing, so it is very important that you and he are well prepared and have 'done it all before' the big day. Water trays, sometimes painted 'swimming-pool blue', often catch horses out, so add this to your list of fences. They rarely contain water, but have startled the unwary on many an occasion. Even Olympic medallists have been seen sailing through the air when their young horrified horses stopped dead when confronted with such an apparent horror!

JUMPING A COURSE

All the training in the world will be quite useless if you cannot apply that knowledge to riding a course of fences, and many people forget the importance of this.

Once you are in the ring you are out there on your own with a mass of things to think about and do in a very short space of time. First and foremost, you must remember NOT to start before the bell. You must instill the right degree of confidence and obedience into your horse so that he approaches his fences happily and under control in order to negotiate them successfully.

You must be sure that your turns into and away from your fences are balanced and controlled, that at all times you are making the most of your arena to reach the fences in the best possible way, and that you end by going through the finish.

Ring practice is terribly important and the more you have the better you will become at actually competing. It hardly matters what the standard is so long as it is not above what can be expected of your horse, but the more you can do to perfect your technique in the ring, the better. Learn by your mistakes, however simple they are – store them up so that you do not make the same ones again.

Riding indoors will make you realise how quick you have to be to balance your horse and how important the turns and impulsion are in a confined space. Outdoor riding teaches you how easy it is to lose concentration, and get sloppy going round the big ring, with all the outside distractions. Concentrate on the job in hand, which is to do the very best possible during that time in the ring and during preparation of yourself and your horse before you go in there.

STRIDES AND DISTANCES

Most people get worried about strides and distances, what to do about them and how to do it, particularly in relation to combination fences.

The horse's stride varies very much, depending on its size, degree of training, speed, and type and on the state of the ground, but speaking very roughly the average horse's stride in canter is around 3.5m (11–12ft).

Combination fences have one or two non-jumping strides between the different elements and these need to be looked at carefully when assessing how to tackle combination fences such as doubles and trebles. When there are three or more non-jumping strides between two fences or combinations of fences this becomes known as a *related distance*. Anything much more than five non-jumping strides can be discounted.

The rider must learn to know what strides to take between fences and then to ride his horse so that these are easy to achieve. A short combination will require a steady, balanced approach so that the horse can easily put in the necessary one or two strides. A long distance will need stronger riding so that the horse is encouraged to stretch out his stride in order to cover the longer distance with ease.

The following chart gives an idea of average non-jumping strides between fences.

No of non-jumping strides	Distance (metres)
1	7–7.5
2	10–10.5
3	14–15
4	17.5–18.5
5	21–22

To achieve consistent clear rounds it is very important that horse and rider are able to jump combinations and related distances with ease. This will only be achieved through practice. Your trainer will probably make you jump a series of combinations at one or two strides, such as one stride to an oxer to a vertical or whatever. It is also very helpful to get used to riding into short distances and long ones so that you are quite accustomed to shortening and lengthening your horse's stride in the ring as you approach the fences. If you have practised well at home and your horse is obedient and confident this should not present any difficulties, but it is one of the prime considerations for the jumping horse. Horses that fight or hollow coming into their fences will need further schooling before they can be successful, and it is worth looking into the bitting arrangements to ensure that you have the best to suit your horse.

TURNS AND CIRCLES

Turning into a fence correctly can win or lose a competition. It is absolutely essential that the horse can turn and circle in balance and remain supple so that he meets his fences correctly and is able to jump from whatever spot you desire.

This is a lovely photograph of the rider balancing her horse around a turn – so very important for the showjumping phase, where the next fence can be won or lost in the approach. The overall impression is one of lightness and harmony. The rider is sitting very well, using her leg to push the horse together, and her hands are nice and soft. The horse is well balanced and prepared

Practise cantering small circles from a bigger one. Really push the horse together and shorten his stride, then push him on a bit and then get him back again. It is terribly important to be able to move forward into a fence and to be able to shorten the horse's back so that you can, if necessary, put in an extra stride or miss one out and thus gain time.

Your horse should be cantering well on both reins and be able to do circles easily if you have worked hard enough on his flat schooling. He must also be able to turn into a fence correctly and some tight turns are a must, so you need to practise these. Really shorten your horse into a balanced 'bouncy' canter with a half halt or two and then turn him, keeping him together and with the correct bend, the way you want him to go.

A good exercise is to have a couple of fences set up about a metre or two off the outside track and to practise turning into these. Another good way of mastering turns is to canter up an inside track about 5–8m from the main track, then turn into the corner (making sure, of course, that you do your turn towards the leading leg), and keep the horse moving so that it shortens up and really uses its quarters to balance and carry itself out of the turn.

CONTROL

The rider must have the correct amount of control to be able to jump successfully and this becomes vitally important when you get to the cross–country. The horse should be obedient to the rider's aids, but must not be overbitted or frightened of what it has in its mouth. It is always best to start with the snaffle and cavesson noseband and then, if you cannot control the horse enough, try the different snaffles such as a French link or Dr Bristol bit.

Nosebands such as the flash, grakle or drop can make quite a difference, especially if the horse opens his mouth a lot and stiffens his jaw. The grakle helps to prevent the horse crossing his jaw and can really aid control in certain situations.

In theory the various types of roller bits stop the horse taking too strong a hold, and copper rollers are the mildest. The Magenis, cherry roller and Cornish (or Scorrier) snaffles are all fairly severe but in the right hands can be very effective. Always remember that soft hands make a soft mouth. Pulling and tugging will only make the horse more resistant and strong as he sets his jaw to evade such treatment. Very often a milder bit can work much better, and rubber and plastic bits have come right back into fashion.

My top horse Warrior was very strong indeed and I used to ride him in a cherry roller, which he loved. I had to learn to leave him alone between fences as he hated to be interfered with, even though he would gallop along with his head virtually on the floor. It was quite unnerving approaching a fence at speed like this, but he knew best, and so long as I did not pull at him he would always shorten himself up before a fence. It took me a year to learn to ride him and we tried everything to get his head up – unsuccessfully! There are times when you must learn to adapt to your horse, especially if you are lucky enough to have one as brilliant and foot-perfect as Warrior, who carried me to wins at both Badminton and Burghley.

For the really strong horse the gag can be the answer but the rider must remember that this works by increased pressure on the poll and an upwards pressure on the mouth, and a continuous pull will gain little response from the horse. There must be a take and release action to get a good reaction. The rubber gag is particularly popular and many horses go kindly in this.

The pelham in its many variations is good for encouraging the head to lower and can be used either with two reins or with roundings and a single rein. The curb chain will govern the severity of this bit and should, in theory, be set so that when the rein is pulled the angle of the bit is at 45°. Curb chains may be double-linked, made of leather or elastic, or covered by rubber.

The double bridle can be used by experienced riders and is by far the most versatile. With its two bits it is possible to raise the head on the snaffle rein or lower it with the curb. However, this is not always as easy as it sounds. In the hands of those who do not fully understand it the bridle can be very severe, and is best left to the experts.

Martingales are extremely useful in giving extra control and the running martingale helps with steerage as well. There are various gadgets such as the Market Harborough, which can be helpful in preventing the head from going up too far out of the angle of control.

It is always worth thinking carefully what your particular problem might be and then discussing with a good saddler and your trainer whether a certain bit, noseband, martingale or gadget will help. For a competition do be very careful and check that whatever tack you are using is allowed. Some tack is allowed for show jumping but not for eventing and it is up to you to check this out carefully before competing.

FLYING CHANGES

The flying change is a must for the show jumper and is helpful for the event horse as well. It enables the rider to maintain a good rhythm and balance throughout, without breaking into a trot to get onto the right leg to approach a fence. In speed classes it obviously saves time, and of course it looks much more professional.

To teach a horse how to do a flying change, he must first be going in a balanced manner and forward on the bit in canter. A pole can be placed on the ground and the horse circled in a figure-of-eight over this on the centre line. The rider must give the aids for a flying change just before the pole and change the bend to the other side.

Remember to balance the horse with a slight half halt and then ride him forward as you shift your weight a little to the other side, changing your leg and hand aids at the same time. The pole will make it easier for the horse to change leg, but this may not be necessary with an experienced dressage animal, who may have learnt to do flying changes by a greater degree of collection and a lighter forehand than is generally required for the jumping horse.

LOOSE SCHOOLING

Loose schooling is a wonderful way of teaching your horse to jump and learn by himself, whilst at the same time enabling you to see how the horse actually tackles the fences, and how easily he assesses them and learns from his mistakes.

If you are lucky enough to have a jumping lane close by this is a great bonus, but if not you can set one up yourself in a suitable school with good fencing round the outside. It is important that there are no places where the horse could get caught up or escape from the lane. He must be guided in and then encouraged forward, with a whip if necessary, but should not be chased. You want him to improve his jumping ability, not to think about the person driving him over the fences.

Start with quite small fences until the horse realises what is expected of him. Once they are sure of this most horses enjoy themselves and the fences can be raised a little at each session. After three or four sessions the horse is usually jumping quite high and you can watch if he uses his head and neck over the fences and brings his withers and forearms up well to clear the jump, as well as seeing how he rounds his back.

Lungeing over fences can also be helpful but there is always the risk

Lungeing is an essential part of any basic training of the horse. For the eventer it can be used not only to correct faults without the weight of the rider, but also as a different means of exercise and to get rid of high spirits before serious work begins. The use of side reins prevents the horse getting out of control, and reduces the risk of knocks should the horse really buck around

that, however hard the handler tries, he cannot help but interfere slightly with the horse's jump. Also some trainers feel it is a bad thing to jump horses on a circle continuously, even without weight on their backs.

Certainly lungeing adds a little variety to the horse's life and it must be a good thing for the rider to be able to study his horse's technique over a fence from time to time. As with all training it should never be overdone. Remember that lungeing or loose schooling are useful for some horses but may not be good for all, especially those that fool around too much or are disobedient to the voice, and they are certainly not essential. Some horses get quite silly and excited, whilst others are very calm and take it all in their stride.

Try to have varied fences in your jumping lane, uprights as well as spreads, and it is never a bad thing to have a ditch if possible. The sooner the eventer gets used to holes in the ground the better, and any cross-country practice possible now is a very good thing.

JUMPING AIMS

It is worth stating in this chapter exactly what you are striving to achieve with your jumping training. The eventer is supposed to be a good all-rounder, able to do a decent dressage and jump a round of show jumps of up to advanced standard, as well as be a good performer across the country. With dedicated work on the flat, time should eventually produce a reasonably obedient, supple and fluent dressage, which will be extremely helpful when it comes to jumping. To jump correctly it is essential to understand the three main parts of the action. Basically these are the approach, the jump and the landing, and each one directly affects the other.

THE APPROACH

While it is not necessary to get too engrossed in a lot of detail, the rider must try to be consistent in all the work done over fences. The leg must be firmly on the horse with the weight pushed well down through the knee into the heel, and this must stay in position and not

This horse is not making the neatest jump over this fence as he has not really brought up his forearms, nor lowered his head enough. A true parallel with the rider sitting a little more upright might be the next step. The hands could go forward a little more to encourage him to stretch and lower his head and neck

These two parallels are set to encourage the horse to use himself a bit more than in the previous picture. Although the horse is jumping better he could still improve his technique. Shortening the distance might encourage him to bascule more over his fences

flop backwards and forwards. The leg must be effective in controlling the impulsion and balance but also be ready to drive the horse forward if it is lazy or reluctant, so that it arrives at the point of take-off ready to spring into the air.

It is up to the rider to decide on a line and speed. The goal should be to get the horse to the middle of the fence with the correct amount of impulsion and speed to jump it easily. The hands should be controlling the impulsion without excessively restricting the forward movement, but the horse must be able to increase or decrease its stride according to the rider's leg and hand aids.

The rider's weight should be slightly forward but never so much so that he gets in front of the forward movement of the horse; nor, for that matter, should he be so upright that he is behind it. He should remain in balance throughout, with his eye on the fence and with the hands controlling, but just before the point of take-off these hands should allow the horse to stretch his head and neck to find his take-off point. The wrists and fingers must be soft and supple so that they are able to follow through as the horse takes off.

THE JUMP

As the horse thrusts into the air it will bring its hind legs well forward to propel itself upwards and forwards, lowering its head so that the shoulders can come up and thus using itself to best advantage over the fence. The rider must remain in total balance with the horse throughout the jump, keeping his weight out of the saddle and not allowing himself to get too far forward. The hands must follow forwards so that the horse has complete freedom to stretch his head and neck as much as he requires and the rider's legs must remain on the horse with the heel the lowest point.

The horse will stretch itself out and tuck up its front legs as it flies through the air, lowering its head so that the withers are momentarily the highest point, and it will round its back over the fence if it has been well schooled and the rider is not interfering with its jump in any way.

THE LANDING

As the horse lands he raises his head and neck and the forelegs stretch out so that he lands first with one (usually the outside) which takes the weight, followed by the second, and pitches forwards as the hindlegs come down to take the weight off the forehand. It is most important that the rider sits up well at this stage and does not increase the burden on landing. You must then allow your upper body to go forward as

the horse gathers itself up for its first rather clumsy stride on landing, and must ease the reins slightly so that the horse can regain his balance and momentum as he resumes his canter in readiness for the rest of the course.

In a combination it is particularly important for the rider to sit up and be ready to drive forward again in perfect balance so that there is no interference with tackling the next fence, and the horse is helped onward by immediate efforts from the rider. Freedom of the head and neck, and driving aids from the rider's legs to keep the momentum up, are what is required through a combination with the rider staying in balance throughout each jump.

The success of each jump depends very largely on the rider, who really must understand what help is required by the horse to leap each fence clear. There will always be the odd horse who is a little careless or lazy, but generally it is the rider who causes the horse to either knock in front on the way up or behind on the way down. Very often only a very slight adjustment is necessary, such as a little more freedom with the hand or a little more weight down into the heel so that the horse can keep in better balance. You may well be getting your

This series of three photographs shows a young horse negotiating two steps. The horse looks confident if slightly questioning, but is maintaining a good forward movement. The rider is in an excellent position, able to ride on forward but maintaining exactly the right balance through the two elements

weight forward a little too much with the result that you are getting in front of your horse – a very common fault – or sitting too upright on the approach and having to make too big an adjustment in the air, which unbalances the horse at a crucial stage of his jump. Ask your trainer what is causing the problem and set about putting it right.

ANGLES

There are occasions when your horse will be expected to jump over a fence at an angle, particularly on the cross-country, and it is worth practising this in an arena to give your horse the idea before having to perform the action over a solid cross-country fence. You may also want to angle fences in the jump-off of a show jumping round. The horse must feel confident about this and the rider must be positive with his riding towards the fence when jumping on the angle.

A useful exercise for angled jumping is to have a small parallel placed across the centre line of your arena at X and ride over it off a figure-of-eight. Make quite sure that your horse understands what is required the first couple of times, and then increase your angles so that you are eventually coming in from a really acute angle. If the horse is balanced well and between your hand and leg the jump should cause no problems.

When doing this exercise practise landing on the correct lead for the direction in which you are about to go. Slightly shift your weight to the side on which you want the horse to land and ease your hand out a little in that direction to encourage that leg to be put down first. It will become second nature once you have mastered the art.

CHANGING DIRECTION OVER FENCES

Another exercise, which is particularly useful for the rider who is having difficulty being independent with the hands, is to make a little course up one side of the arena where the rider has to steer the horse from one direction to another and then back over three or four small fences. The secret here is for the rider's hands to remain independent and not become fixed on the neck. This would effectively block the horse's neck, making it impossible for the animal to change direction. The inside rein with the rider's outside leg will guide it in one direction, then the outside hand must take over with the other leg to push it in the opposite direction. The other hand must remain soft and able to go with the movement of the head and neck, and never be pulled back. The jumps should remain very low as this exercise is more for the rider's benefit through increasing his coordination, than for the horse. Never make the angles too difficult to start with until horse and rider understand what is expected of them.

If you have been able to practise all the exercises mentioned so far in this jumping section, your horse should be quite handy and well prepared to cope with most courses to be met in the ring – so long as you have jumped some fences a little bigger than those actually to be met in the competition. You always want to be sure that you are jumping things at home bigger than those to be met in the actual show, as with all the razzamatazz of the event the horse may well not be concentrating fully and it is so important that all goes well on the day if confidence is to be built up.

WALKING AND ASSESSING THE COURSE

It is very necessary for the rider to walk and carefully to assess the course, particularly bearing in mind the horse you are to ride. If it is a young one, you must think of making every approach as easy as possible, getting straight for everything and giving the horse the best help you possibly can. Ride him strongly past any spooks and let him see round the arena by getting in there as soon as possible.

Walk your distances carefully and think how best to ride them, taking your horse's stride into account. Note the position of the start and finish and whether you would do best to go inside or outside certain fences to get a good line at a jump. Be ready to guide the young horse firmly past the collecting ring – he may try and hang towards it, knowing that is where he came from. Study the ground; is it hard or soft? Sticky ground will hold a horse and so he will need riding on a little stronger. On very hard ground the horse may not want to jump out too much, so he will need driving on a bit between the fences.

Is the course built with good solid materials, or is it very short of filling? In the latter case most horses tend to get a little careless. Is the ground level? If on a slope you may gain ground going downhill and get too close to the fence or, if going uphill, a little too far away, so you need either to hold the horse together more or drive on a bit.

All these thoughts need to be taken into account so that you can get in that arena and do your very best, regardless of whether you or your horse or both are young, inexperienced or veterans. One thing that is for sure is that you will only succeed if you take everything into account every time, and do your very best each time you compete.

CHAPTER 5

Cross-Country Riding

For most event riders the cross-country is the favourite phase. It is the enjoyment of riding fit horses over solid and imposing fences which makes worthwhile the many hours, days, weeks and months of building up muscles, confidence, endurance ability and general training. Nothing is better than at last being able to put all this into practice and gallop a well prepared horse round a demanding course of fences. It is a wonderful feeling, difficult to equal, when you have built up a special partnership with your horse and know that you can trust each other over often awe-inspiring obstacles and enjoy every minute of it.

Perhaps it is the anticipation, or the slight feeling of danger, or the achievement of the ultimate goal you have set for yourself, or just the sheer terror of riding over fences that rarely budge, or possibly the competitive urge to jump the course better than anyone else to help yourself win which makes it such a special phase, but to most competitors this is the part that matters and that makes up for any disappointments in the dressage and show jumping.

Because the cross-country is important it is worth learning about every aspect of this riding skill, so that you can set out round the courses confident that you have prepared yourself and your horse in the very best way possible to tackle whatever is presented. The fences are solid and must be respected and it is up to you, the rider, to treat them accordingly so that you and your horse negotiate them safely, sensibly and, hopefully, successfully. There are numerous different types of fences and new ones appear annually, but generally they are variations on a basic theme and the following types represent most of those to be found on today's courses. I will try to cover the basic points to consider when jumping these obstacles.

Captain Mark Phillips – four times winner of the Badminton Horse Trials – jumps out of the water at Gatcombe on Cartier. Water must always be treated with caution, and it is particularly important that the horse sees that there is a fence to jump out over. The rider must keep steady enough not to create too much spray

This young rider has just survived a tricky moment. His horse took a huge bold leap into the water over the log pile. The rider is trying to turn his horse to the right, where the jump out of the water is situated. He is looking where he is going, and you can clearly see him pushing the horse round, using his left leg

FENCES

Uprights/Verticals

These straightforward fences should present few problems as long as the rider remembers to sit in the safe position, with a strong lower leg and with the weight never getting too far forward. The horse must not be on its forehand but driven forward into the hand, and not allowed to get too close nor stand off too far away.

Always ride straight at uprights, be accurate and avoid getting too close to them. Post and rails give the horse a chance to see through but walls and palisades, upright sleepers etc mean that he cannot see the landing, so be prepared for a slightly cautious horse to slow down and lose impulsion into these fences and to compensate by strong use of your legs.

Some uprights are placed on top of a hill and it is important to ride very strongly at these so that the horse has the necessary impulsion to clear them neatly. Some are placed at the bottom of hills or on the way down, and with these you should sit up well on the approach and keep the horse together so that he does not launch himself too soon and land with a jar which could demoralise him for the next fence.

Some uprights, such as Helsinki steps, are built into the sides of hills and need accurate and positive riding. Choose the most inviting step and then ride confidently and with control straight at your chosen spot.

Upright bounces require an accurate and balanced approach with the horse contained well back on its hocks to make the fence easy to jump. Coming in too fast is asking for trouble, but too slow an approach will make the fence too much of an effort for the horse. As with all uprights it is important that the horse is neat in front and snaps up evenly with both front legs. If the horse is inclined to dangle his legs you should practise over high cross-poles to try and improve his technique, and when riding cross-country keep a firm even feel on the reins.

SPREAD FENCES

Plenty of impulsion is required when jumping spread fences and care must be taken not to stand off too far, thus making the fence even wider than it is already. Do not approach too slowly but with enough pace to make the fence easy. Always jump parallels straight and with the horse up off his forehand.

Some spreads, such as large logs or tables, may have rather false ground lines but so long as they are solid and imposing they rarely cause a problem, because the horse as well as the rider has naturally a healthy respect for such solid-looking jumps.

Hedges are often quite wide. They can really be ridden at strongly and certainly should be if they have a big ditch on the landing side. An open ditch on the take-off side rarely causes a problem so long as they are ridden at straight and with plenty of impulsion.

If confronted with a spread off a turn, be sure to ride at it hard and allow the horse to take all the rein he needs to clear the fence with ease. There is nothing worse than seeing a horse land on the back of a wide fence because the rider has not learnt to 'slip' the reins or at least give the horse its head and freedom to stretch when necessary. Nothing demoralises a young horse quicker than being restricted over a spread fence, so do make sure the juvenile or inexperienced horse has plenty of impulsion and pace coming into a spread.

Ditches

Few fences cause as many problems as ditches. Whether this is due to a psychological fault on the part of the rider, the horse or both is difficult to determine but it is very important to get your horse used to ditches from the word go. Start over little ones and really ride at them, kicking all the way and being sure to give the horse freedom once he has taken off so as not to catch him in the teeth. Sometimes, if your horse has a real horror of ditches, it is helpful to school him with an experienced animal in front but he must then do it on his own and be made to jump as many ditches as possible regardless of shape or size.

There are numerous fences incorporating ditches, from simple ditches to trakehners, tiger traps, and coffins, which are almost a fence in their own right. With a coffin it is important that the horse is sufficiently athletic to be able to cope with the upright in, a jump over a ditch which is usually in a dip, followed by an upright out. It certainly requires a bit of practice to master the art of popping in and out of a coffin on a young horse, partly because there is a lot to think about in a short space of time.

Big ditches such as 'graves' need very strong riding as you want the horse to jump right over, so he needs riding forwards and upwards. Big trakehners also require positive riding and if the rail is angled across the ditch it makes for a nice groundline if you can jump it where the ditch is towards you. Hedges with ditches in front need strong and purposeful riding but usually jump very well.

Tiger traps often cause a few stops because they can look a bit 'spooky' to a young horse, especially if the approach to the fence is uninviting. Keep the horse's head up a bit and ride strongly forward, thinking and looking ahead. This is important with all ditches – never look down into them but always up and over the other side. Some ditches have a rather poorly defined take-off rail in front of them, or none at all, which may look rather off-putting to the rider. However, invariably the horse is quite capable of seeing this for himself and anyway takes off further away from a fence than one thinks, so this lack of definition very rarely causes problems.

American former double World Champion Bruce Davidson sails over these parallel bars in his distinctive forward and 'very-close-to-the-horse' style

This horse is giving the solid table fence plenty of height. Table fences are often quite imposing and need riding. The rider is in good balance; her lower leg is quite secure and she is looking straight ahead to the next fence on this schooling session

These sloping rails over Windsor's big ditches hold no fears for Lucy Challis and Private Eye. Wider fences should always be attacked boldly so that the horse stretches out well and is able to clear the ditch (should there be one) with ease. There is nothing more demoralising for the horse than being held back over big fences

If there is a big ditch on the landing side of a fence which the horse will not see until it is airborne, such as after a big hedge, it is best to get fairly close to the fence on take-off and ride the horse strongly, giving well with the hands over the fence so that he can stretch out well for the landing. Sit up and keep riding forwards in case the landing is poached or liable to give way.

Banks
Banks appear on many courses and are presented in a variety of different ways, from single ones to big Irish and Normandy banks to double banks, but all require the necessary impulsion to get onto them and then the balance and control to get off them. For these obstacles the horse's stride needs to be shortened and the horse itself collected together, to prepare it for the effort required to get on and then off. Really push the horse forward into the hand so that he has the impulsion right underneath him, ready to be released as he springs up onto the bank. Generally speaking you should keep the speed up, but it

depends on the size of the bank. Small ones where you go on and then straight off do not require as much effort as a big Irish bank, which will steady one on top anyway and then require a bold leap off.

Normandy banks require quite a bit of speed and impulsion as generally they are jumped as a bounce, on then immediately off over a rail depending, of course, on the distance at the top. Banks with a rounded top will slow the horse down as he will be a bit unsure how to cope and when it is best to jump off.

Double banks need plenty of impulsion and the rider must keep up the momentum all the way through. Ride hard over the first one, sit up well on landing, and ride hard at the next.

Steps

Like banks, steps need riding at boldly, especially those going uphill. The more steps there are the more impulsion you will require, so be sure to ride strongly but with your horse bunched up together so that the energy can be released as he jumps up from one step to the next.

Jumping from a height requires balance and boldness, especially if there is another jump to come. Karen Straker, team silver medalist at the Seoul Olympics, is well balanced here, with a good straight line from the bit to her hands and elbows. She is maintaining forward impulsion with her legs so that the horse does not land too steeply

Windsor Three-Day Event winners, King Max and Mary Thompson, jump economically over this downhill log. Fences on a slope are best jumped like this so that the amount of jarring to the legs is kept to a minimum. If approached too fast the horse will land much further on down the hill. However, the approach must be sufficiently determined to ensure a successful jump, so don't get caught out!

Two steps are relatively easy so long as your horse has practised them before. If not you should preferably start over one, just popping on and off a few times, then progress to two. If you can practise over three that is a bonus.

Remember it is very important not to get left behind going up steps, so push your weight firmly down into your heel and push up from your ankle, knee and hip joints as the horse jumps. Never let yourself get behind the movement of the horse as he goes up, but keep forward and in balance. Whatever happens maintain the forward momentum. Do not stop pushing on the first step, keep riding all the way.

Steps down can look quite daunting but if your horse has learnt how to pop on and off steps when schooling these should not be difficult. The main things to remember are to keep straight, sit up well on landing, and get the horse moving forward so that he jumps out reasonably well and does not pitch too deep onto his forehand. Make sure you have a strong lower leg over these fences, or you may get into difficulties. Spectators love to watch people have near misses, and anyone rather loose in the saddle over this type of fence may well get into the 'Going, going . . . gone!' situation if they are not in a safe secure position throughout the obstacle!

Remember that when jumping uphill you will tend to get a shortening of the horse's stride, so extra momentum will be required; whereas downhill you may gain ground and therefore must keep the horse steadied. Steps down are generally best approached in trot so long as the horse is going forward well.

Corners

A corner fence will require an accurate and straight approach. Generally speaking it is best to take a corner at right-angles to the apex but each fence will need assessing individually to decide which line would be best, having taken the going, the approach, and the terrain into account. Move back a few strides and study the fence and choose a point well beyond the jump to guide you on your approach. Remember this landmark and ride towards it when the time comes. Look carefully at the alternatives so that you are sure where to go should the ground deteriorate etc before you get there.

Remember not to get too close to the apex in case you run out, or too far in so that the jump becomes impossibly wide. Accuracy and an obedient horse are the keys for these fences to be successfully negotiated. Once on your line to a corner, ride forward with purpose. It is a big mistake to steady into this type of fence as the horse will tend to wobble and change direction, so think and ride positively and strongly forward towards your chosen take-off spot.

Combinations

Combination fences require control and accurate riding and test the athletic ability of the horse, especially if there are several elements. It is very important to plan your route and then to ride every stride through this obstacle. Far too often people give up half way through a fence, leaving the poor horse at a loss to know what is expected of him. Combinations often look daunting and confusing to a young horse, so it is very important that you approach the fence in such a way that he can work out what is expected of him and see a way through. At all times be positive, keep the horse balanced and keep up the impulsion.

It is very important that the horse comes into the fence nicely

This horse and rider can be seen taking the quick route through a combination fence, jumping the corner. Corner fences require accurate riding and course-walking beforehand. It is best to divide the angle between the two rails, and to aim to jump the imaginary divider at right-angles. It is vital when walking the course to also walk the alternative routes, so that if something goes wrong and you do not jump the fast route ie 'plan A': the corner, you can instead jump 'plan B', and go the slower route

balanced and, generally, not too fast. His hocks must be underneath him and he must not be on his forehand, so sit up on the approach and push him together as you will probably have been going quite fast over some straightforward fences before reaching a combination. If you have angled fences incorporated in your combination make sure that you know exactly where to jump in order to give your horse the best possible distance, and approach at a sensible pace to be able to give him sufficient space in which to achieve this.

Combinations going downhill require a balanced, steady approach, so do sit up well and get the horse back off his forehand as you come into these and then keep hold a little more than usual throughout. Any combination going uphill will require extra impulsion to help the horse keep up his momentum, as required for the 'out' of a traditional coffin.

Jumping into dips and pits can be quite frightening for the horse, especially if the problem is exacerbated by the 'light-into-dark' factor. Because a horse's eyes adjust from light to dark less quickly than a human's, it is sensible to set the horse up well so that he is fully aware of what is expected of him. Ride your horse on very positively, in case he is scared by what can look (to him) like a very dark void as you approach the obstacle. Horse and rider seem confident here, and are in good style over this fence

Amelia Wood on Benjamin Bunny, jumping this fence in the water accurately and confidently. The picture demonstrates clearly how much spray can be generated by the movement through the water, and it is therefore important to steady the horse on entry so that he will focus on whatever is in front of him, without being blinded by the spray

Karen Straker and Corriwack, negotiating a rather unusual combination fence. This involves a very balanced approach over a big upright, followed by a jump onto a bank over a gaping chasm, then a drop off a bank, a stride, and over a second big upright. Over this type of fence it is essential that the horse is held together in a nice, bouncy stride, so that it has enough impulsion to make a series of athletic jumps

Bounces will require a very controlled approach with the horse being brought well back, so that he resembles a coiled spring. Very stiff horses find this type of fence quite difficult so keep hold of them and push really hard with the legs to help these horses cope more easily.

Water

Water always requires thought on how to ride it, the speed at which to approach, and how to cope with any fence that precedes the water or is otherwise involved.

There seem to be two different ideas on the best way to ride water. In America the riders are generally taught to go faster into this type of obstacle than we do here in Britain. Certainly this is a good idea if the horse can jump out well, the water is not deep and there is not too much of a drop. However, very often the water is on the deep side and there is quite a drop down into it. If you have ever run into the sea you will know what a 'drag' you get and, while it is all right for the actual

Ginny Leng, World and triple European Champion, on Griffin, lining up for the jump out of the water at Badminton. She is keeping Griffin in trot to reduce the amount of spray created

A dramatic leap out of the water by 1990 Badminton Champion Nicola McIrvine and Middle Road. The horse has made a big effort to bounce out of the water onto the platform, and then over the upturned boat. The rider does her utmost to give him freedom by throwing her arms forward

landing, if the water is deep this drag can really pull you down on the next stride. Always sit up well and keep a firm hold of the reins, push your legs forward and get the horse's head up as soon as possible on landing.

If there is a fence to be jumped in the water it is best to come back to a trot to allow the spray to settle and the horse to focus on the fence. Cantering through water creates a lot of spray which can impair his vision. This also applies to a step or fence out of the water. Once you know the horse has seen the fence, keep hold of him and ride him strongly at it.

It is important to know the depth and state of the ground in a water jump so a careful inspection will be necessary beforehand. A firm even landing is what you are hoping to find, where the horse will feel safe

---

Clissy Bleekman and Delphy Dazzle taking a bold leap into the lake at Badminton. The rider is sitting well back, keeping a feel on the reins with a secure lower leg. The horse's face seems to be saying 'Yippee, let's go!' – although I don't know if the rider shares his enthusiasm!

102

and not peck on uneven ground. If the landing is soft and uneven you must find the best line through, approach steadily keeping a good hold on the horse's head and sit so that you are fairly upright and braced ready for any necessary action. Do not forget to use legs firmly throughout, and strongly enough to get your horse into the water whatever happens. A good strong trot or bouncy canter is generally considered the best pace in Britain. It is the pace of approach and the reaction of the rider on landing that are the two most important factors.

If possible watch the experts at the different types of fences and notice how they balance their horses with the minimum amount of adjustment to the horses' strides; their position into, over, and away from the fences; and the rhythm they adopt round the whole course. Watch·them at combinations and over the uphill and downhill fences, over verticals and spreads, and how they ride their different horses in different ways. It is the ability to adapt to horses, courses, ground, and levels of fitness which makes such a difference and is vital if you want to be successful.

ASSESSING COURSES

Having learnt how to jump the different types of fences it is important to think of the course as a whole and how each fence relates to the next. The course-builder will have set various problems requiring such things as boldness, caution, agility, control and speed, as well as jumps designed to suit the different types of horses and their short or long strides. Some fences may be easy for one type of horse but difficult for another, and this is the factor that needs careful consideration. What will your horse find easy or difficult?

Long galloping stretches followed by a combination fence will require a lot of control, whereas a twisting and turning period through trees will make the horse alert and probably nicely balanced ready for a

Different experiences at the same obstacle: an awkward moment for Ian Stark and Sir Wattie, who have got rather close to the take-off. Ian is, however, in a safe position for the drop landing. It is fatal to lean forward or allow the lower leg to slide back over a drop such as encountered jumping into water

Mark Todd and Charisma, however, in perfect style: control, balance, neatness, a safe position and superb technique. Mark and Charisma were gold medallist at the Los Angeles Olympics in 1984, and the Seoul Olympics in 1988

tricky obstacle. The more awkward fences tend to come in the first two-thirds of a course when the horse is fresh, then generally ease off a little towards the end, but every course-builder is different; some favour upright fences while others prepare the nice groundline type of course. Very often there will be a fence designed to prepare you for something later in the course, such as an easier corner option before a more difficult one which would take you right off course if you did not tackle it in the straight way described previously.

Remember that your young horse needs as much experience as possible. There may be certain fences on the course which would give him vital experience if jumped in certain ways; however, always remember that you are trying to build up confidence too. If he has jumped two or three awkward fences it may be best to keep to straightforward routes through fences near the end of the course, so that he finishes feeling pleased with himself rather than a little worried. It will pay dividends on your next outing.

If you are the one needing the experience and have a horse who has done it all before, this is the time to go out and tackle the more awkward options on a course. In this way you will build up your own confidence, know that you can do it, and discover which fences feel easier to jump than you had at first feared. Keep the basic advice of riding on at a spread and steadying a little for an upright and combinations in mind.

Watch other horses round the course if you can, and particularly when they finish – this can tell you a lot about whether the course is taking much out of the horses or not, and will help you to decide on what pace to try and set if your horse is ready, fitness-wise. Also look at fences you are worried about: watch the pace and how people ride it to make it easy to jump. However remember, when it comes to your turn, to set off knowing that this is what you have spent all those hours, weeks and months working for, and it is up to you to think about every fence as you approach so that you do not let yourself or your horse down by doing anything you will regret.

Ride each fence as you planned on your walk round and, at the end, think back and see if your assessment of the course was about right. If it was not then you still need to learn quite a lot more either about yourself, your horse or courses in general. Without wanting to sound depressing, I find that after over thirty years I am still amazed by certain fences seeming either ridiculously easy or 'simple' ones turning out to be really quite difficult!

SPEED

Acquiring the speed necessary to ride round cross-country courses in near to the optimum time requires a great deal of experience. Several factors affect how you can achieve this and there are times when it is best simply not to try, but a competition is there to be won and if this is your aim you must evaluate everything and then set out to do your best to achieve it.

A steady rhythm, with the rider using shorter leathers to be able to balance and control the horse better, is the first priority. Looking at the most direct route from point A to point B and keeping up a steady flow into and away from your fences are the most important aspects of riding cross-country. If you try to bear in mind that every time you take a pull you are losing a second it may help to stop you reining in. The horse should be pushed into better balance and never pulled into it. If you cannot achieve this you are either not riding from your leg into the hand enough, or your control system is inadequate and needs further thought.

The inexperienced horse will need to be taken round the first few event courses fairly steadily to give him time to work out what he is to do, and to gain the necessary experience and confidence. As these grow he can be pushed on a bit quicker and learn to jump accurately as well as faster round the courses. It is the ability to lengthen the stride rather than go quicker which actually increases the speed in most cases. Never go faster than the speed of which your horse is capable at his stage of fitness. As he gets tired towards the end of a course, so he will also become less capable and neat; so hold him together and only expect as much as you feel he can give safely until he is really fit.

The fastest rounds are invariably the ones that look effortless and easy because the rider has got his horse going forward in a controlled but long stride, meets his fences right and wastes little time over them. Galloping flat out round a course will only wear your horse out, usually results in some very anxious moments which do nothing for the horse's or rider's confidence, and can result in bad falls. You may achieve a fast time round some courses in this way but it is consistency that counts in the end, and there is no way that very technical courses can be won with this sort of riding. Clear rounds are what matter and speed with caution is what cross-country riding is all about.

The state of the ground will inevitably play an important part in how you can ride the course. Soft ground will be slower and more tiring, whereas firm ground can be slippery, so the horse should not be over-pushed.

107

TACK AND PROTECTION FOR CROSS-COUNTRY

With all the work that goes into getting your horse fit and training him for dressage, show jumping and cross-country, it would be stupid not to protect both him and yourself adequately for the most demanding phase. A silly knock can put your horse out of action for days, so if possible it is well worth preventing this when schooling. Do not forget the essential points, such as whether your horse is adequately shod for a cross-country school or competition. It would be foolish to go if the clenches were up, the shoes worn and therefore giving no grip, or if the toes had got too long so that unnecessary strain was being put on the tendons. You will probably want studs, so check that your farrier has put in stud holes – especially if it's your first school of the season, when you may not have had them in for some time – and take studs with you to use if necessary.

Check your tack carefully, especially girth buckles and stitching on reins etc, and ensure that you are happy with the state of the leather, particularly where it gets a lot of wear. Make sure your reins are safe and that you have the non-slip type of your preference for good control. Do not forget to have the right bit with you for cross-country, plus any different nosebands, martingales etc to help with the brakes if these are a problem.

A breastgirth or breastplate to prevent the saddle slipping back is essential and the overgirth or surcingle, to hold everything in place and act as a safety girth, is also a must. A clean numnah under the saddle to prevent any sores is important. The numnah must be in good condition and smooth, so that it does not wrinkle up and cause a scald.

The legs need protecting and clean supple boots, of whichever type you normally use, must fit well and be secured with safe straps or buckles. Plain velcro alone is not enough to keep boots done up, so if these are all you have use tape for extra security. Do remember that the tape must never be tied too tight but at the same tension as the boot strap, so that it does not cause uneven pressure on the legs.

If bandages are used put them on over some good padding. Apply the bandage evenly and firmly down onto the fetlock joint and back up again, securing with a knot on the outside of the leg or velcro and tape, or by stitching the bandages in place which is generally the safest.

Bell or overreach boots prevent the horse getting bruised heels or overreaches. There are various types, but try to avoid having those with a large buckle which can get caught up on things. The best are the pull-on sort but these are not the easiest to get on and off, and so they do need to be the right size for your horse's foot.

The rider's protection is equally important and it is compulsory to wear a crash helmet or cap in competition. Make sure that your harness is easy to secure and comfortable.

A stock or hunting tie is sensible even in hot climates, as not only does it support the neck but also protects it from nasty cuts should you get hit by branches etc. This can easily happen should you get slightly off course. Your stock pin should always lie horizontally so that it does not go into your chest in the event of a fall.

Back protectors are compulsory in some countries and are certainly recommended. The waistcoat types are light and comfortable even if they do tend to be a bit hot. Make sure that yours protects your spine and sides as well as allowing plenty of freedom for arm movements. The protectors are wonderful for preventing the bruises that one dreads after a fall and they have saved thousands from serious injury.

Leather boots are strong and protective and should always be worn for cross-country. It is helpful to have rubbers in your sitrrups to prevent your feet slipping. Make sure that your stirrups are the right size for your foot, and are made of steel and not nickel, which can break. This, of course, also applies to your horse's bit and to all buckles.

Your stick, which must not be longer than 76cm (30in) should have a flat top which will not poke into your eye. Some narrow-topped types have caused quite nasty injuries so do get the safer sort. Many riders twist some elastic bands round the tops of their sticks to prevent them going through the hand and this does help you to keep hold of it.

Sweaters or polo-necks with long sleeves, even in hot countries, will give extra protection to arms and prevent scratches etc. Many riders find they get quite badly grazed arms and certainly if they hit the ground this is the case, so a good cotton polo-neck in hot climates and a warm woollen one in the cold are advisable.

Gloves are a must and the non-slip variety are excellent for wet weather wear. It is always worth having at least two pairs handy. The 'pimple' gloves have revolutionised the horse world and really do mean that you have good grip at all times.

RIDING SAFELY

No amount of protection will be any good if you do not think and ride safely, according to the training and experience of your horse and the ground and weather conditions.

CHAPTER 6

The Competition

PLANNING

Having done all the preparation for the first event of the season, as this draws nearer the feeling of anticipation becomes intense. Whatever you do, do not make the classic mistake of panicking at the last moment that your horse is not fit enough. Many is the time this has happened and the poor horse has suddenly found itself being galloped flat out twice instead of once or taken out for an extra hour of hillwork in the days just before the event. This usually results in the horse getting uptight about the change in routine and stiffens him up so that he comes out aching and rather unco-operative, which then demoralises the rider more and the whole thing falls apart!

Above all, keep to your normal exercise routine. Ease off a little on the schooling over the last week, just give a little warm-up jump two or three days before, and do 20-30 minutes suppling and dressage exercises. It is often a good idea to run through your test once or twice so that you know how it feels with your horse, but do be very careful not to do this too often or you will have your mount anticipating. If you are having any difficulty with certain movements practise these out of sequence with the rest of the test.

Be very careful not to get frustrated or cross with the horse. It will only make him more tense on the day. Better to go off for a good long hack and then come back to try something for 10 minutes, than overdo it and make an issue of something trivial. Remember the horse is probably very fit by now and longing to do something just as much as you are so extra patience, however difficult, will pay off later.

Plan well ahead and make sure that everything you are going to need at the event is ready, in good condition, and has been thoroughly checked, especially if it has not been used for some time. If necessary make lists of everything you want to take especially at the beginning of the season when you have become a little rusty about what you use.

Start by thinking if you are to stay away for a night or two. In America, with long distances to travel, you usually find the event takes two or three days anyway whereas in Britain sometimes all three phases can have been completed within 2 hours. On the other hand you may find you have long gaps in between the phases, or that you do dressage or even dressage and show-jumping the day before the cross-country.

Make sure you include bedding for your horse if necessary, plus enough food and hay. If he is sensitive to a change in water it is wise to take a big container with you for the journey and possibly for your stay. Do not forget your own mucking-out tools. Check your tack carefully to ensure you have enough of everything, plus a spare bridle and other bits and pieces for replacements. If you have two saddles it is worth taking them, even if just to keep your best one clean and tidy for the actual event. Several numnahs are a must as are towels, scraper, buckets and sponges for washing down.

Your plaiting and stud kits must be fully stocked up with everything necessary, including a spare set of shoes and a first-aid kit

Everyone has their own preference with regard to saddles. Ideally both a dressage and a jumping saddle are required. The straight flap of the dressage saddle will help you look more the part in the arena, while the forward flaps and knee rolls help to ensure a good jumping position. Strong safe leathers, steel irons and rubbers in the stirrups will also aid a secure seat while jumping

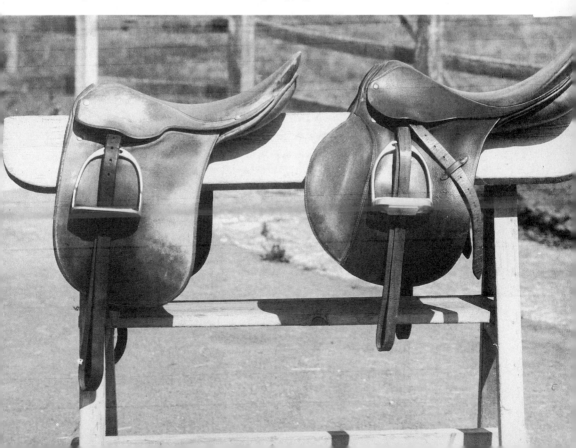

This rider is correctly dressed for junior and novice eventing in a tweed coat, and with a well secured crash hat for jumping. Her position is fairly good, although a little more weight down into the heel would have put her leg in a better place. She is going forward well with her hands but maintaining a good contact ready for landing. She is already looking ahead for the next fence

with anything you may need for simple problems and for poulticing – remembering to have a good pair of scissors! Enough coolers, rugs, waterproofs etc should be put in to cover every eventuality, especially for the unpredictable British weather.

Your own personal kit must include the correct clothes and hats for all three phases, which means there is quite a lot to remember with hats, boots, breeches, coats, back protector, and goodness only knows what. Do not forget the omnibus schedule to tell you all the details plus your confirmation letter, flu-vacs and any other necessary certificates for the horse, as well as number cloths or bibs and dressage tests – and always have a good map so that you can find the event!

The following checklist, divided into different groups, may be a useful guide.

1 General kit for travel or staying away: bedding, hay, haynets, water buckets, water container, food to last plus a little spare, feed bin, supplements, salt, electrolytes, dustbin for soaking hay if necessary, travelling gear including headcollar and rope, rugs, travelling boots and bandages, tail bandages and guard, roller, poll guard if used, sweat rugs or coolers, mucking-out kit, skip or muck sheet.

2 Stud box: to include studs, tap, nails or probe to clear out holes, spanner, spare set of shoes. Plugs of oiled cotton wool or similar to fill up holes.

3 Plaiting kit: to include plaiting thread, blunt needles, elastic bands (if used), scissors, and knife or 'quick-un-pic' for unplaiting.

4 First-aid kit: to include dressings, antiseptic, cotton wool, a bowl for bathing, wound powder, antiseptic cream, poultices, scissors, bandages and padding plus any other favourite remedies. Americans are allowed to administer and carry far more drugs than the British so needles and syringes with appropriate drugs could be included.

5 Tack: to include bridles, saddles, girths, irons and leathers, numnahs, breastplate or breast girth, martingales, overgirths, spare bits and nosebands. Weight cloth and lead. Brushing boots, overreach or bell boots, bandages and padding with fastenings, tape. Saddle rack, tack hooks and hammer.

6 Washing down kit: with buckets, sponges, scraper, body and foreleg wash if used, towels, sweat rugs or coolers. Spare set of bandages and pads to put on after cross-country.

7 Rider's clothes: to include hats for three phases, dressage and show jumping coats, stocks and pins, gloves, shirts, breeches, boots, spurs, whips, back protectors, wet weather gear, hot weather gear, kit to walk course, stopwatch.

8 Flu-vac or passports: information on the event and stabling, rule books.

The above can be adapted to suit each individual and the standard of event being entered, but it covers most of the necessities for all types of event.

TRAVEL PREPARATIONS

Once you have decided what is needed get it all prepared and packed up the day before you want to leave. Check that the truck or lorry is full of fuel, water and oil, and that tyres and lights are all in good shape. Do not forget to include the trailer or gooseneck in your check.

This horse is well protected and ready to travel, with knees and hocks covered. A tail bandage will prevent rubbing, but horses travelling for a long time are best left without a bandage in case this is applied too tightly, in which case it can interfere with the circulation. The number of rugs required depends on the weather, and how much the horse sweats. It is sensible to put the horse in a good quality halter with a strong rope

Depending on the event, you may need to ring for your times the night before or get them from the secretaries' caravan the day before the competition starts. Make sure you know how to find out this information and have your number, section and class at hand to tell the secretary. If you cannot run for any reason always remember to withdraw by ringing up and confirm this in writing, giving your name, number and class section.

Having prepared your horse for the journey according to the weather, with well protected legs and tail, allow plenty of time for travelling. It always takes a little longer to get started than you expect and you invariably find the traffic is worse than you thought. Freeways and motorways are much more restful for the horse than lots of twisting and turning on narrow roads. If it is these latter ones that you have had to travel along the horse will certainly need half an hour to relax and settle at the other end before you start getting him ready.

Never underestimate the effect the journey can have on your horse, especially if you plan to do everything in the day. Good smooth driving with sympathetic use of the brakes and accelerator makes all the difference, but some horses do not travel terribly well and take quite a lot out of themselves on the journey. These animals will benefit greatly from not being rushed at the other end. Younger horses certainly do not want to be whisked out on arrival and then have a flurry of activity all round them, which will get them really wound up and excited. Quietness and a calm atmosphere will pay off when you want to go out and produce your very best in the dressage arena.

ON ARRIVAL

If you are arriving the day before, it is worth getting settled in first, finding out where everything is, and possibly even walking the course once before riding and working your horse. Sometimes it is best to ride around quietly for half an hour followed by 20 minutes or so of dressage. Other horses are best loosened up and then worked quite hard for however long seems necessary, before relaxing quietly on a loose rein until he is dry and ready to go in. Some horses even benefit from a bit of a jump, but do be sure you do this according to the rules of the competition and with your crash hat on and fastened.

However frustrating it may seem, do not expect your horse to go as well at the competition as he does at home. This very rarely happens until the horse is fairly advanced and the rider is really relaxed and experienced at competing. Having said that, there are always a few who rise to the occasion and do very much better under pressure than anyone ever imagined from seeing them at home!

It is important that your horse is settled, relaxed and happy when you bring him back from working, whether you are not competing until the next day or have come back to have a tidy and brush-up before going off to do your test. However silly or overexcited he may have got, do make a point of ensuring that you are friends by the time you have finished, so that you go off next time in the right mood.

If you are stabling during the event allow time to find and get to this facility, if it is not actually on site. Be a good guest and leave

117

everything neat, clean and tidy when you depart. Replenish water containers and reorganise yourself so that everything is easy and prepared for the next morning. Remember to feed your horse in plenty of time and cut down on his hay the night before he has to gallop. He should not have any hay for 4–6 hours before he gallops. In hot weather generally give a little less food, but keep offering water in small amounts up until 1 hour before jumping or galloping.

ON THE DAY

Arrive in plenty of time. You will have been able to work out how to plan your day having learnt of your time. Make sure your helper, if you have one with you (and everyone should have someone around just in case anything untoward happens), knows what your times are and how you intend to go through the day. It is quite a good idea to pin up your times etc in a prominent place so that everyone knows them and is reminded what is due to happen when.

If you intend to walk the course again before you ride be sure to check at the secretaries' tent that there have been no alterations to the course, or that the ground conditions have not changed unduly overnight. This is particularly likely with British courses and may result in a change of plan about how you ride a certain fence.

Make sure, as you walk for the second time, that your original plans still seem to make good sense. Sometimes other options become obvious as you get more familiar with the course. Look closely at your approaches to the fences and take in landmarks that could be useful to you as guides to fast routes etc from one fence to another. Be sure there are no turning flags to go round; you must always keep a red flag on your right and white ones on your left. Check at combination fences that you have planned to jump through all the elements marked in between the flags. Some can be a little confusing if you are not careful.

Be sure to check your finish carefully. It can be easy to go the wrong side of this at the end of the course when your eyes are watering and you are elated by finishing. Make absolutely certain that you are clear which flags mark the finish.

Walk your showjumping course early in the day, as you are unlikely to get much of a chance to do so later on. Study your approaches to each fence, work out strides in the combinations and how you will ride them, especially if they seem on the long or short side. Look at your start and finish and before you jump make sure you know what the bell to start sounds like.

THE DRESSAGE

Allow yourself plenty of time to prepare for the dressage and once you get down there discover as soon as possible which is your arena. Report to the steward in good time so that he knows you are around, and then concentrate on relaxing, suppling and working your horse in for his test. It is worth using brushing boots during your warm-up just in case the horse is a little fresh and knocks himself, but be careful not to excite him when you take these off and have a final polish. Much better to do as little as possible and keep him calm than to make him look immaculate and then do a dreadful test. If you have been warming up with a stick, be sure to drop this before going into the arena.

There are times when some horses really get uptight and start to become very overexcitable. This is often due in part to the rider, probably unwittingly, tensing up on the horse. Do keep calm, whatever happens. Try taking the horse's mind off things by twisting and turning quietly, circling, allowing him to stretch down well, and then pushing him forward into contact. Walking a tense horse occasionally works, but as soon as you try to do something different he may get silly again, and you are back to square one! Keeping your horse busy and occupied is normally the best advice. It will help both of you.

Try to think purposefully of what you have been trying to achieve during your training: a smooth, obedient test with good transitions from one pace to another, well shaped movements, straight entry and exit, an easy rhythm with lengthening clearly defined when required. Accuracy is also important if the judge is to be able to give really good marks. Mentally prepare yourself to do the test by thinking through it and riding it in your mind, and by telling yourself that this is the moment you have been waiting for to present your training to everyone. Sit up tall and look the part, and when your turn comes get on round the arena to allow your horse to get accustomed to the sights. Breathe deeply, relax and just concentrate on what you have got to do – no more, no less.

When the judge's horn or bell goes, take your time and give yourself room to make a nice turn so that you are straight and on the centre line a few strides away before entering the arena. Come to a smooth halt and remember to smile at the judge – he or she has a long day ahead too!

When you have completed your test and left the arena allow your

This young rider is achieving some good lengthening as she pushes her horse forward during her test. She is, however, riding up out of her saddle, having no weight in the stirrup; she has rather stiff arms, and is poking her head a little. It is important to achieve a correct position and to learn to be effective early on in your training

horse a reward of sugar or even a small handful of grass if he has stayed calm and relaxed. If he has become tense or excited it is worth going off straightaway to work him for another 5-10 minutes before bringing him back to the box, so that he learns what to expect: a reward if he is good – more work if not.

THE SHOW JUMPING

It is always a bit difficult to warm up satisfactorily at a competition because there are usually only a couple of fences to use and everyone else wants them at the same time. It is, however, very important that your horse is prepared properly to give him the best chance of doing a clear round in the ring. More horses are spoilt at this time than people realise, because they are asked to jump fences before they have been warmed and suppled up and, very often, are given a bit of a shock with all the other horses milling around. It is very easy to undermine confidence at this point so keep your jumping to a minimum, and keep the horse happy and confident by not asking him to do anything too big just before going into the arena.

A cross-pole to start, then a few verticals and a couple of spreads should be ample. Try to jump off both reins and vary your jump by coming off a shorter or longer turn into the fence, rather than making it too big for your young horse.

If you are on your own you may have to wait for some like- minded person to start their horse off in this way and then join in. If you have your own helper they must be quick at altering the fences, and know what you want and what the rules are on practice fences. If your horse is not going too well and is rather overawed by the occasion keep the fences small, ride him strongly in the collecting ring, then get into the main ring and get his mind on the job away from the distraction of the others and think and ride with determination.

It is quite difficult to determine when to do some practice jumps, but it is better to be a bit too early than too late. You probably need to be going into the practice ring 20 minutes before you want to jump because it may well be 10 minutes before you get near a fence. At least if you have warmed up you can keep your horse walking round and just pop over one fence if necessary before going in, but if you are late it may be impossible to get to the fences at all.

Before your turn comes watch a horse or two round the course to refresh your memory and to see how it is riding. Listen to the start bell so that you know what you need to hear when it is your turn, and work out if people have been getting any time penalties and how to avoid getting the same. It may be that some people have been going around rather than inside a fence, or they may have been going too slowly, or the course was simply measured tight and you must keep going smartly all the way round.

Just before your turn comes, trot and canter your horse around so that he is alert and ready for the occasion. Take him calmly into the arena as soon as you can so that you have time for a good sharp canter round before the bell goes. Always be positive and get in there meaning business. Make the most of your arena, get straight at your fences and really ride around your turns into or away from the obstacles. Wait for the bell and be sure to go through the start and finish.

At the end of your round pull the horse up, walk quietly from the

121

arena and reward him. If, anything major has gone wrong it is best to pop him over the practice fence a couple of times at least but save any further schooling for home, when you can take time to analyse what and why things went wrong and put it right before the next time.

In Britain the show jumping is normally done before the cross-country, except for one or two championship classes. Consequently, of course, the horses are generally fresh for the show jumping and more as they would be for a schooling session at home. In America, however, show jumping (or stadium as it is often called there) is generally done after the cross-country, and your horse will be feeling quite different having already had the busiest part of his day. He may be quieter and in some ways more settled, but may also be a little stiff especially if it has been a hilly course or a hot and humid day. How much this will affect him depends very much on the horse and the time-gap between the two phases.

If show jumping is preceded by cross-country you must be careful not to overdo the warming-up stage, as the horse will in effect already have had this on the cross-country, but he will need quite a lot of walking to loosen up well and then a few pops over practice fences to get his eye in and remind him that accurate jumping rather than speed is required now. You are likely to have to hold your horse together as the exertions of the previous two phases will be beginning to tell.

CROSS COUNTRY

Preparation for the cross country starts with the tacking-up stage. First check that you have the right studs in for the ground you are going to ride over. Everyone has their own preferences but the general rule is to have small sharp ones for hard and slippery going, and large ones for soft ground. Check that the shoes are in good shape and that there has been no spreading nor any nails come up during the day. If so, call for the farrier to attend to this right away.

Overreach or bell boots should be put on next and then the horse should be tacked up with everything except his bridle. Check that your breastgirth, surcingle, girths and saddle are all set in the right position with the numnah comfortably arranged and pulled up into the front arch of the saddle. Many people, so I am told, unplait their horses for this phase so that they can grab hold of the mane in emergencies!

Once you have got everything ready and prepared, attend to the legs. Whether you use boots or bandages is entirely a matter of preference, as there are pros and cons for both, but it is generally better not to put these on too early as they need to be firmly applied and it is best not to have anything like this on the legs for longer than necessary. Remember to keep bandages even and firm all the way down onto the fetlock and back up again. Stitch or tape them at the same tension as the bandage on the outside of the leg and never the inside, where they could get knocked or brushed by the other leg.

If boots are used make sure all fastenings are done up at the same tension with straps facing from front to back so that they do not catch on anything. They should be put on so that they are firm enough not to slip down or around but not so firmly that they are overtight and liable to hinder circulation.

The bridle can be put on last. A shoelace or similar attachment should be fastened between the top plait and the headpiece of the bridle to prevent this disappearing should the rider have an unfortunate fall and push, or try to push, the bridle and himself off over the horse's ears!

Keep a lookout on the time as you need to be down at the start 10 to 15 minutes before you are actually due to be in the start box. Before mounting make sure you, as the rider, have everything you require. Your back protector, gloves, stopwatch if carried, crash hat, stick, and spurs must all be in position or with you as you get on.

Many people like to grease their horses' legs as extra protection and this should be done by another person so that you do not get it on yourself. Place the grease over knees and then on down the front of the legs and joints, then behind from the stifle joint over the hock, down the front of the leg and over the fetlock joints including the boots or bandages. The idea is that, should a horse get trapped or caught up in any way, it will be able to slide over or out with less likelihood of cutting the skin. There are various preparations on the market but udder cream was the original favourite being cheap, greasy and fairly easy to wipe off afterwards. Whatever you use needs a thorough washing with soap to remove it, which can be an on-going performance!

Once you are ready walk your horse down to the start, check that everything is still running to time, then loosen up your horse quietly for 5 minutes. Give him a couple of strong sharp canters and one or two jumps over the practice fence. Do not overdo him, as you want to conserve his energy, but make sure that he is well awake and has his mind on the job in hand. You should always report to the cross-country steward as soon as you arrive at the start area but, once

Karen Lende (USA) and Lutin V at Burghley. Burghley Three-day Event is immensely popular, and always attracts many foreign competitors. The horse seems to be enjoying himself; the rider is in a good balance with a secure lower leg. Notice the thick grease smeared on the fronts of his fore and hindlegs, which will help him slide over a fence should he get into trouble

warmed up, check girths and stay within call, walking your horse around. Run through your course in your mind as you wait.

When called to go to the start box, wake your horse up with a short trot or canter and go quietly to the box. At this point be careful not to let your nerves get the better of you so that you relay anxiety to the horse – keep him quietly walking around until the starter counts down. You do not need to be in the box until about 15 seconds before the off if it is likely to cause your horse to get overkeen.

Sometimes horses will go in and be quite happy standing looking out backwards – others are best wandering in and out on a circle – some will stand quietly anyway, others go right over the top in their anticipation of the big moment! Keep calm, keep them moving, and then only at the very last moment turn them towards the first fence and stand for a moment before the signal to go is given. If you use a stopwatch start it just beforehand, but few worry about such things until they reach advanced levels. If you are worried about the start, it is worth mentioning it to the starter and telling him what tactics you intend to use so that he is in the picture.

As you go around the course remember to ride your fences as you had planned, giving the horse the best approaches and coming in at sensible speeds. Keep up an even rhythm and hold him together throughout, rebalancing for combinations and upright or downhill fences and keeping hold but riding on at spreads, steps, banks etc. Remember to count the fence numbers and watch for turning flags! Try to keep the momentum going through water, but not too fast, and as you come towards the finish make very sure that you go through the right set of flags. Pull up gradually on a firm rein, keeping the horse together until he is back to a walk.

Dismount at a safe distance from the finish area and loosen girths, overgirths, and the horse's noseband before walking him quietly until he stops blowing excessively. Take him back to the horsebox and untack him. Depending on the weather wash him down and scraper him off, doing this two or three times to help the cooling process if it is very hot. If it is cold be careful about washing down too much, especially over the back or you can cause muscle spasms. In either case do not let the horse stand for too long, especially if he is still blowing, when he should be kept walking quietly with a cooler or sweat rug on. Always be careful washing down with cold water as it can be quite a shock to the system of a hot horse. Try and pour it into buckets early so that it warms up during the day.

Boots and bandages should be removed as soon as possible and the legs massaged and checked for any obvious cuts or bruises. Once the horse has stopped blowing and is relaxed, take out studs and bandage his legs carefully using either dry bandages or a poultice. Some people prefer to poultice routinely after the cross-country, others just in front, others not at all. Personally I think it depends on the going and ground and how demanding a course it was for your particular horse and his legs. At this stage it is better to cosset the legs for 24–48 hours if you are in any doubt.

Never let your horse get cold by being left in a draught, even if generally it seems quite warm. He may be better inside rather than outside the box if this is likely to happen. Also remember that, as he cools down, so his temperature will gradually drop and he may well get cold later on, so check him regularly to see if he needs an extra rug or blanket especially in colder weather. In hot weather keep him as

American Sandy Clarke on her elegant horse Free Scott jump the log in Huntsman's Close in beautiful style

cool as possible and either park in the shade or at least open every possible ramp, door and window so that there is a free flow of air.

Offer frequent small drinks of tepid water after the cross-country once the horse has stopped blowing. A quarter of a bucket every 10 minutes or so until his thirst is quenched should be offered, and then half- to one-hourly after that so long as the horse is not to stadium or show jump afterwards. In this case give him no more water for an hour before he jumps, and then go back to offering it. Remember that in hot weather horses quickly become dehydrated, so alway be sure to have plenty of water to offer throughout the day.

As soon as your horse is happy and relaxed and has stopped blowing, but not before at least three-quarters of an hour since you finished the cross-country, he can have some hay. He will be pretty hungry by this time and longing for some sustenance. He could have his haynet whilst you attend to his legs and studs. A little later on he might like a small feed. Keep it small as he will inevitably be tired and you do not want to make his stomach work too hard, especially if the journey home is still to come.

Check over your tack, make sure you have everything back with you and tidy it up. It is much easier to rub it over straight away if you have time so that it is clean when you get home. Store everything away with any bits that you still require easily accessible.

Before you put your horse away in the box walk him around a bit to see if he has stiffened up a lot or looks uncomfortable in any way. He may well look a little stiff for the first few strides but so long as this wears off quickly he should be fine for the trip home. If you have any worries, or your horse looks uncomfortable, it is better to call for the vet rather than wait to get home when a small worry could have become quite major. Your horse will thank you for a comfortable journey, with a suitable painkiller if necessary.

When you get back home or to the event stables make your horse comfortable, give him a small nutritious feed, and leave him to relax and rest. Check him last thing before you go to bed. I always leave bandages on for that first night as a bit of extra support and as warmth to encourage a little more circulation to ease any sore spots.

If you find your horse 'breaks out' in a cold sweat, which does sometimes happen, a little walk round and gentle rubbing of the ears with your hand helps to warm them up. A towel or your hand may help to dry off over his loins etc if he is quite damp. Change the undersheet if necessary. Sometimes two or three changes are required.

After all this you can think about a little celebration, and savour the success of the day! So long as nothing too disastrous happened you can be satisfied that things are moving in the right direction. Rosettes will not necessarily materialise on the first few outings, but if you can see that they could easily be within reach, with some improvements in your performance, then you have done pretty well. If you have had a disaster, remember that there is always another day when things could be much better, and learn by your mistakes. Just occasionally success is immediate – if it happens to you, make the most of it!

THE FOLLOWING MORNING

When you go out the following morning look at your horse and see what he is telling you. Is he bright-eyed, cheerful and looking rather pleased with himself, which is what you should find all being well?

If that side of things looks good remove the bandages, wash off any poultice and, if all looks satisfactory, leave him to eat his breakfast. Later, see how well his legs look once they have cooled down from having the bandages or whatever on overnight. You really need to leave them a good hour and then have a thorough feel to see if they are a pair, preferably cool.

Lead your horse out and walk him around for a few minutes and then jog him up. If all is well you can feel pleased and let him have a good quiet amble on a hack or go out for a little in the paddock to relax. Treat any minor bumps or bruises but if there is anything you are worried about, or that looks worrying, it is better to call the vet for professional advice before you do anything detrimental which could put the horse back weeks in his work.

Analyse your day, think over where things could be improved and try and see what you learnt from the experience. Hopefully you will have built up your own confidence and be all set to do even better at your next outing.

Clean and check over all your equipment and get it all put away ready for the next event. Give your horse a few easy days to settle and relax from his exertions, so that he comes back into full work roughly three or four days later. Give him a good bran mash the day after and then build up his feed again. He will inevitably have lost a bit of weight and probably 'tightened up' with the run, but he should have filled out again after a couple of days.

CHAPTER 7

Further Training for Horse and Rider

Having done a few events with your horse you will be getting an idea of how he is progressing and be starting to think of more advanced competitions. There are numerous championships for which to qualify and it is fun to aim towards one of these if you feel it could be something worthwhile; or you may wish to start thinking about riding in a three day event.

To do this you will need to have the right qualifications for the standard of event you are hoping to enter and it is important that you plan ahead to get these in plenty of time. Inevitably you will need to improve your standards so that you can achieve more. Further training therefore becomes essential and it is particularly important that the rider keeps learning more, so that he can always be working a stage ahead of the standard at which he is competing.

You will have seen from the comments on your dressage sheets what areas need working on for this phase. Ask yourself what overall impression the judges are getting and whether they like it or not. I am afraid all judges have different ideas on what they like to see but, after a few tests, generally you will get a picture in which certain words keep cropping up, and you should take notice of this and work out what it is that needs to improve.

DRESSAGE WORK

The following are the most usual comments. You can decide which applies to you and what you should be doing to improve. You may find one relates to another or that there are a series of little things which all lead to one and the same result.

Overbending
This is a common problem and needs to be dealt with early on. It usually means that the horse's poll has dipped downwards and is no longer the highest point of the neck. It may also mean that the horse is

dipping its nose backwards and is not going forwards.

This problem can be dealt with by stronger riding forward with the leg into a softer hand. Very often the horse overbends in order to escape the rider's strong hand. Think therefore of lightening the hand, as well as questioning whether you require a thicker or softer bit to encourage the horse to take a little more rein.

Raise the hands momentarily as you push your horse strongly forward. Sometimes a good medium trot two or three times round the school will help the hocks to work more and so the head should rise. This problem can result if you have ridden a lot in an arena and have not ridden the horse forward quite enough. Work for a few days out in the field where there is more room.

On the Forehand

This means that your horse is rather front-heavy and is going into the ground, so you will need to lighten the front end with more positive riding from behind with your legs. Keep a contact in front and literally push the horse's hocks underneath him to raise his head.

Young horses are often 'on the forehand' because they have not matured enough and still have some growing and strengthening to do. In this case you may do more harm by trying to get the head up than by leaving it at this stage, as with correct training the horse will gradually come up naturally as he matures.

Work on transitions to improve the balance of the horse, and generally keep him alert and help him use his hocks more by twisting and turning. Once he strengthens behind he will be able 'to come up in front'. Working up hills should also help. Be careful that you do not get too strong in your hand or you may find your horse starting to overbend, thus creating another problem!

The position of the rider can play an important part so make sure that you are sitting up well when riding dressage. If you have brought the horse on since he was young, you may have ridden him leaning forward to keep the weight off his back and never sat up properly since. This shift in the weight can make a big difference.

Stiffness on Turns and Circles

This can be caused by tension or insufficient training and lack of suppleness. Some horses react to atmosphere and tense up when they go out and therefore do not perform at their best in the test. Others go well outside but tend to 'drop a shoulder' on turns in the confines of the arena.

A nice medium trot across the diagonal. The horse is balanced but moving forward well and extending the stride. It is important to work at lengthening and shortening and to ensure that the horse remains even and on the bit when changing pace

The tense horse requires a lot of work before he will settle and perform at his best. If you feel he works fairly well at home it may be worth lungeing him first at the event. It can have a soporific effect, quite apart from wearing him out a bit.

Pole work, over and through the poles, should help to create more suppleness. Turns and circles on both reins, transitions from the different paces, and lateral work will all help.

Probably the most important aspect, however, is the rider's aids. Are you using your inside leg strongly enough on the girth to make the horse bend around it, and are you asking for the flexion with the inside hand and just supporting with the outside one? So often riders tense up themselves and become totally ineffective in the ring. This, of course, is quickly communicated to the horse, especially in the competitive atmosphere.

Horse Not Engaged

This is another comment which usually means that the horse is not coming through from behind to propel himself forwards correctly between the rider's hand and leg. The hind feet do not track up into or over the footprints of the front ones. This suggests to the judge all sorts of faults in basic training.

It may be caused by tension, so a lot more work before the dressage test may be required. Suppling exercises to relax the horse's back would be helpful and pole work, serpentines, turns and circles all help to create softness. None of this will work, however, unless you are applying enough leg to make the horse use himself more behind. A stronger leg is essential and the horse must be driven forward into a soft but restraining hand. Imagine you are holding a spring and are pushing it together from both ends to increase the tension.

By riding in this way your horse's increased activity should solve the problem so long as he is going forward strongly. Keep riding him forward into medium and extended trots and then bring him back again, pushing his hocks underneath him each time. You must keep thinking positively forward with all your training but sit up, allow your horse to carry himself with freedom, and do not block his forward movement by tipping forward yourself.

Horse not Straight

Straightness is one of the most difficult things to achieve, partly because the horse's quarters and therefore his hind legs are broader than his shoulders and his front legs! How straight a horse will be in the arena depends very much on how he is ridden, and whether he is more stiff on one rein than the other. It is certainly not unusual to find that the horse goes better to the right or left – after all we are mostly right- or left-handed. What is difficult for the horse is to turn down the centre line and keep going forward straight without wobbling or stiffening on the one side, thus creating crookedness.

The European Championships: Rodney Powell and the Irishman II enter the Trout Hatchery, over the big drop, in a good safe position. It is vital that the rider sits up well and supports the horse in preparation for the next, crucial stride, when the horse has to readjust its weight and get used to the depth of the water. If this is on the deep side, and the rider gets out of balance, disaster could well occur!

Trotting poles being used here to practise riding straight. The horse is wearing tendon boots and overreach boots for protection. The rider has a soft, allowing hand, with a strong leg pushing the horse forward over the poles, and is looking well ahead. The diagonal pairs of the trot step are shown clearly, and the horse is moving well through the middle of each pole

---

(top left) The loneliness of the roads and tracks phase is demonstrated here by Lucinda Green on Mins Lincoln at Chatsworth, 1987. This phase is designed as a warm-up before the steeplechase, and to allow the horse time to recover after it, before the horse has its 10-minute break and sets off around the cross-country course. Lucinda's six wins at Badminton, on six different horses, is a record unlikely to be beaten

(left) New Zealand's Tinks Pottinger and Graphic, jumping out of the water at Gatcombe in excellent style. The horse looks alert, confident and full of running, even though it is nearing the end of the course. Notice the strain put on the girths by the breastplate, which is used to prevent the saddle slipping too far back. Gatcombe is an extremely hilly course, and the use of such safety measures is vital

Generally, if you push the horse forward he will straighten. If he is hanging onto the one rein it is necessary to take more feel with the other hand and soften the hard side by vibrating the corresponding hand a little. Keep your hands supple and practise riding up the centre line. Also practise riding 2m in from the track, keeping your horse between hand and leg. Some horses miss the outside boards and keep trying to hang towards them.

Shoulder-in is very useful in encouraging the horse to supple up and can be used to great advantage, especially if the horse is made to bend to the stiff side. Once your horse is less stiff and not tense he should go a lot straighter. Make sure you are keeping your hands soft and not restricting the horse with one hand. Bad habits on your part are more than likely the cause of any problem the horse presents.

Quarters-in

This usually refers to the horse bringing his quarters to the inside of the track when in canter. A common fault, it is generally caused by lack of engagement of the hocks which are not bending sufficiently to be carried underneath the horse but instead are going sideways. If the horse is not pushed together enough this fault will present itself very early. The horse has got to be collected up more, pushed together with a stronger leg into the hand with a series of stronger spurts in canter, and then made to come back to a more balanced pace. Canters to walk and up into canter again off both reins will help.

A little shoulder-in at canter is an excellent movement for this problem but the horse really must be back on his hocks before you can attempt it. Until your horse improves you may need 'to think' shoulder-in when you ride in the arena in order to correct this problem in front of the judges. Only ask for a light bend, get the shoulder just to the inside and then ride forward. Sit up straight yourself, do not collapse your inside hip and keep both legs on the horse to keep him going forward and straight.

Inaccurate riding of movements

This fault is inexcusable except when your horse is playing up. If you have learnt your test correctly and know what is required and where, then you really should not be throwing away marks by not riding accurately.

Your circles must be round and of the right size, not 12m if a 10m one has been asked for, etc. A serpentine must be ridden so that each loop is of the same size.

A simple change in dressage means that you come from canter to walk and then strike off on the other leg. You should get nought if you do not do this as you will simply not have performed the movement asked for by the test.

You should lose two marks, even if the judges do not ring the bell, if you have performed something at the wrong marker so do make a special effort to know the arena markers and learn your test accurately. Losing unnecessary marks in what is a highly competitive sport can be very costly.

Riding marks

You may be satisfied that your riding is competent and that you regularly get a six for this, but there are another four marks sitting there which could be awarded if the judge felt you were good enough. It is a well known fact that a few judges do not vary their marks much whoever is riding, but there are a lot more who will give a seven, eight, nine or even a ten if they feel the test warranted it. So why not work on achieving a better mark? Every one counts.

The marks awarded are not just for your position but also for effective use of the aids and general presentation of the test. Study the professionals and look at how they enter, move off, turn and perform their transitions. It should all be easy, calm and rhythmic. How do they cope with an overexcited horse, a very tense one, a lazy one, those with poor basic paces and those that naturally look good? See if you can relate any of these professional performances to your horse and your style of riding.

What comments have you had on your dressage sheets about your riding? Think about what they say, and try to work on improving things. Get your trainer to work on you as much as the horse – it will of course help both of you as, if you ride right, there is a far greater chance of the horse responding more positively!

Riding without stirrups will help to get you down in the saddle so long as you relax down, and do not grip up out of it causing you to perch on top rather than become part of your horse. Lunge lessons are excellent with a good trainer and can work wonders for you. Think of the common faults of looking down, poking the head forward, rounded shoulders and/or back. Loose seat and a consequent floppy leg are common, the toe is often up but turned stiffly out, or the leg is totally ineffective. Imagine yourself as a tree with your legs as the roots. These should be strong and firm and the basis of your whole position – if the legs are right the seat should be good. The upper body

should be erect without being stiff, the arms hanging naturally at your sides with relaxed elbows, wrists and hands. The head should be up and looking ahead and the overall picture should be that horse and rider look the part.

GENERAL IMPROVEMENT

It must be said that the best way to improve is to get a little better at everything all the time, and to consciously think about this whenever you school your horse.

As you aim for a higher standard you will be working on more advanced movements and these will take time to perfect. Work on the

Some horses really enjoy exercising themselves out in the field. This horse enjoying his summer rest has got very fat, and it will take some time to fitten him up for fast work over fences. When assessing how long is required to bring a horse up to peak fitness, look at his condition when soft and let down. A fat horse will take much longer than a lean one

principle of 'little and often', but keep going back to the movement to improve on it until you achieve what you want. If you are having difficulty it may be that you are not giving the right, necessary aids to achieve the right result, so consult your trainer and set about working out how to put things right.

Make sure your horse is being fed enough to cope with any extra demands on him, especially if he is the type that sweats a lot. There are times during training when the horse may need a little more or even a little less food, so keep an eye on this especially if he starts to get a bit dull in his work.

Work out whether the fitness side of things feels right and ensure that the horse is doing enough of this for whatever you have in mind. As the season goes on the horse should be pretty fit and basically will only require a couple of long rides a week, or the occasional fast-work session, in between his events if there has been quite a gap between outings. Keep the horse cheerful by occasionally giving him a couple of days off in the field as a break. It will be good for him both mentally and physically and he will return to work better for the change.

JUMPING IMPROVEMENT

Do not forget the jumping side of things, consider how your horse is coping with the various courses you have ridden so far. Is he consistent with his clear rounds? If not, why is he having a problem? Is it because he is lacking confidence, is not athletic enough to cope with certain types of fences, or is lacking confidence with them? Does he require a different approach, are you tough enough and do you ride him positively enough?

Give all this a bit of thought and see where improvements could be made. It is so important to get everything right whilst the horse is at novice or preliminary level, because once he has progressed to higher things it becomes more difficult to keep confidence and morale good. Sort out every problem as soon as it arises so that a little one does not turn into a big one.

If you have had a little problem on a course somewhere, sort it out there and then if possible by going back to practise over the fence at the end of the event – with the organisers' permission. This would not be wise, of course, if the ground is bad in any way or if the fence was one you felt was asking too much of the horse anyway. It would then be better to go and find a slightly modified version somewhere else. Sometimes it is helpful to jump part of the fence, such as the first part of a combination; then, if it is accessible, jump the 'out' part; and then put the whole lot together.

Combinations very often do cause problems and it may well be that your horse was confused as he came towards the fence and saw an alarming number of poles or elements. However, this should not happen if your horse has done the necessary training and is confident,

Having taken off too far away from the first step, this horse will need plenty of impulsion to enable him to negotiate the second. The rider is in fair balance with the horse and is ready to use her legs to help with the next step, but is sitting down with too much weight in the saddle

so it is much more likely to have been caused by the rider's speed and angle of approach into this type of obstacle. Ask yourself what you might have done wrong. Did you balance your horse enough before the fence to set him up properly for it, did you look for the easiest route and present it to your horse in such a way that it all looked possible?

Go and have another cross–country school if you feel it necessary, but if the horse just had one stop you can usually assume it was something wrong with your approach and the way you rode into the fence. Remember once you are on your line to sit up and ride forward into the fence.

If you feel your horse is not meeting the more straightforward fences right, analyse what is happening and then try and put it right. It may be that you are too far forward yourself and encouraging the horse onto his forehand, so that he is getting too close and deep to his fences. He may be standing off too far and frightening himself a bit, in which case keep hold of him a little more on the approach and push his hocks more underneath him with your legs so that he gets to a better take-off spot. It is very important to keep the leg on all the time in order to achieve both rhythm and good balance into your fences.

TIME

Are you achieving the time fairly well, if your horse has got to the stage of being pushed on around his cross-country course? If you are having problems at this stage, there could be a number of different reasons. Are you wasting time between your fences, or slowing up too much to jump them? Are you riding the course too slowly, or is your horse simply not fit enough to complete the course in the required time? You must aim for an even, established rhythm, which will enable you to do a good time. Remember to take the type of ground and course into account. If it's very hilly you will find the time tight anyway, as you will twisting round through heavily wooded courses, so on these keep up a steady rhythm; but you will not want to go especially fast.

If it is possible to get a video of yourself on the cross-country you will more than likely be able to see for yourself what you are doing wrong and where the time gets wasted.

If you have trouble in the show jumping and are getting time penalties regularly, then it is usually due to riding too slow generally round the course and not getting around your corners quick enough. Ride on a little more between your fences and push your horse together more rather than pulling him back.

RIDER'S FITNESS

Having spent so much time fittening your horse, it is just as important to be fit enough yourself. This becomes even more so as you progress. Far too often one sees unfit riders letting their horses down by flopping about at the end of a course, just when the horse needs maximum assistance by being firmly held together between hand and leg.

You should be building up your own fitness through the riding you are doing in training your horse. This works to a certain standard but you still need extra to make yourself fit enough to gallop round the course and be effective at every fence.

Riding certainly helps to keep your muscles in trim but will only be really effective if you actually work in the saddle. For instance, trotting without stirrups can be very helpful. Start by doing this for 10 minutes and gradually build up to half an hour. Get a professional to watch your seat and hands, and work at sitting down well in the saddle.

Running and swimming are two of the best ways to fitten yourself up and should be done regularly to help your breathing and tighten up muscles. Do not run too fast but build up the work by increasing gradually each time you go. With swimming, try and do a bit more and use your arms and legs hard to thrust through the water. Breast stroke, butterfly and the crawl are good energetic styles. A little underwater swimming is beneficial as it helps to build up the lung capacity. Work on gradually increasing the distance underwater and, with ordinary swimming, increase the lengths up to your target.

Walking is another excellent means of getting fit and, like the horse, if you can find a few hills to go up and down you will quickly feel fitter. Some people get very enthusiastic and use the treadmill, which can be an excellent and quick method if there is one nearby.

Gymnasiums usually have quite a selection of equipment designed to exercise and strengthen certain parts of the body, and if you know you are not strong enough these can be used to excellent advantage. For instance, if you have difficulty controlling your horse, try to build up arm muscles so that you can hold him. I found press-ups very useful, gradually building up to fifteen. It was not long before I was able to keep him under control throughout the course.

Using stairs instead of elevators or lifts in everyday life, walking instead of using the car, bending and stretching on waking, and aerobic classes on the way to or from work will all help. Never forget that your own personal fitness is most important and that you owe it to your horse to be in the best possible shape for the events ahead. I was training as a nurse when I was chosen to ride at the Olympics, so was not able to ride as often as everyone else. I asked the hospital if I could be put on a ward on the sixth floor, so that I could run up the stairs, and I worked up to eight hundred skips daily on the hospital roof as well as going running and swimming. In this way I was able to improve my fitness considerably, and was certainly able to hold my own with my male team mates, which was quite gratifying!

LOOKING AHEAD TO THE THREE-DAY EVENT

If everything has gone well it may be possible to think about doing a three-day event. These are run according to the standard of the horses: novice and preliminary to start with, then intermediate and advanced, with international CCI being the ultimate aim. The top riders then get selected to represent their countries at international and Olympic events.

To ride in a three-day event means you have another couple of phases to cope with, which require experience and practice. These are the steeplechase and the roads and tracks sections, and you should be confident that you know exactly what to do and how to ride them. Experience is important, as it will make the whole event easier to cope with if you can ride round the roads and tracks within the allotted time and be relatively safe on the steeplechase course.

The Roads and Tracks, Phases A and C of the three-day event, are designed to test the endurance ability of the horse. Phase A acts as a warm up for the steeplechase and Phase C gives the horse time to recover from Phase B before he tackles the cross-country. If the horse can relax well doing this phase, it will be enormously beneficial. Keep a close watch on the time as being late at this stage is very costly on time penalties

Roads and tracks

This is the endurance part of the three day event and also acts as a warm-up before phase A, and as the recovery period after the steeplechase. Known as phase C, the longer this is the better as it allows the horse's heart rate to drop right back to within normal limits after galloping round the steeplechase course.

Phase A, the first roads and tracks, is basically the warm-up for the steeplechase and varies in distance according to the standard of the event. It is usually carried out at a speed of 220m per minute, which means that each kilometre (0.6 mile) is carried out at a steady trot or slow canter, taking just a fraction over 4 minutes per kilometre.

To practise for this you can measure 1km (0.6 mile) stretches and get accustomed to the necessary speed. So much depends on the going and type of terrain. In open spaces it is easy to 'lollop' along, but if you have to go through woods or up and down hills you will need to keep going to stay within your time. It is quite possible to go faster on 1km, taking it in say 3 minutes, and then take 5 minutes for another kilometre which includes a steep hill or very rough ground. In the event you will be aiming to bring your horse in as fresh as possible before he either starts round the steeplechase, or comes into the 'Vet box' for a vet check before the cross-country.

It is less tiring for the horse if you can canter out of the saddle so that the weight is forward. Teaching the horse to settle and relax on this phase is the important thing, in order that he takes as little as possible out of himself. Keep a contact but work on getting your horse to trot and canter in a loose and relaxed manner.

Steeplechase

For the steeplechase the horse has to gallop and jump safely at speed over a course of steeplechase fences within the optimum time. This time varies according to the standard of event but at Advanced level is 690m per minute.

The ideal way to train for this is actually to find a few decent steeplechase fences to ride over. If you have a trainer locally, he might well let you have a practice and, if he can advise you on how to ride at speed over these fences, you will find it very helpful. They are usually quite big so need attacking in a no-nonsense way with a firm, consistent feel on the mouth and a firm leg. Your stirrups need to be a few holes shorter but not so short that you lose effective driving power.

Try to set your stride some distance away and then ride for it. You will save more valuable seconds than by checking the horse into each fence. Keeping up a steady rhythm all the way round is your aim, as this takes the least out of the horse and will help to get within the time. Do not forget the aim is to finish just on the optimum time, or up to 5 seconds inside. Anything more than that means you are tiring your horse unnecessarily.

Your position in the saddle needs to be braced a little more than for the cross-country, so keep your legs well forward and support your horse with your hands, which should not give more than is necessary. Bridge your reins on the horse's neck to help give extra support and sit up well so that you do not push the horse onto his forehand on landing.

It is worth having at least two or three practices over some steeplechase fences before your first three-day event but, once you and the horse have mastered the art, it should not be necessary to do much more. If you have not been able to get a practice do not worry too much: a couple of fast jumps over a brush fence, really keeping hold and pushing him on, is the secret. Once you have done a couple out on the course the horse will soon get the message if you sit up that little bit more.

To keep progressing must be your principal objective, so keep thinking forward to whatever you hope to achieve. However, never forget that your horse is only an animal and will need a break every now and then, both physically and mentally. He cannot be expected to be in tip-top form all of the time. When things are going right everyone is happy but of course that cannot last forever, and you must learn to know when it is time to just stop and let the horse relax for a period. You too will need a break at times. Making haste slowly is usually the best method in the long run. If you can work quietly on the basics and really get them right, and never think that you have done enough training just because everything is going well, then you should continue to have a lot of fun with your horse and the sport for many years to come.

CHAPTER 8

The Three-Day Event

The ultimate ambition for every event rider has to be a ride in a three-day event. This is really the big test. It is a combination of dressage to demonstrate the training of the horse on the flat; the speed and endurance phases on the second day, which consist of a warm-up phase of roads and tracks known as phase A and a steeplechase course of between six and ten fences, to be jumped at a speed of between 640-690m per minute, – called phase B; and a second roads and tracks, longer than the first and designed to allow the horse to recover from the steeplechase, known as phase C. This is followed by a compulsory 10 min break to refresh the horse before he is asked to set off on phase D – the cross-country, over anything from twenty to thirty-five solid fences depending on the standard. All this is designed to prove the versatility and stamina of the event horse.

On the third day there is the show jumping, which consists of a single round of show jumps to prove that the horse is in good form after the exertions of the previous day. Before being allowed to start in the competition every horse has to pass the first veterinary inspection to ensure that it is fit and sound to compete. A second inspection precedes the show jumping. The three-day event is therefore a time to demonstrate everything from good stable management to the very thorough training necessary to run in such an event. The overall distance on the speed and endurance phases may be from approximately 16km (10 miles) up to 29-32km (18-20 miles) in a big championship.

Different countries and events will have their own way of doing things but generally the horses are stabled on site, or very close by, and there is a wonderful friendly atmosphere as competitors, helpers and friends settle down to four or five days of hard-fought competition. After the months or maybe years of training and preparation there is something very special about competing in a three-day event.

The excitement of the occasion can affect everyone in different ways. Some go off their food completely; some become very talkative and others rather quiet as they cope with the anticipation of getting started.

THE PREPARATION

Along with the general training of the horse already discussed, the last four to six weeks before the three-day event will have included two or three long hacks, preferably up and down hills, and this will have been interspersed with dressage, perhaps one jumping session, and one or possibly two gallops (or competitions) per week.

If the ground has been very hard or you are worried that your horse is getting a bit 'jarred' then you could try and arrange a few days in the swimming pool. This will rest his legs but keep him working and using his lungs. Remember that this will be a different type of work for your horse and should not be overdone initially. Take care until your horse is used to it.

If swimming is not possible then preserve his legs by avoiding roads and try and work him on the soft. He can canter on large circles in a school rather than gallop on the hard. He can build up fitness like this so long as you really work him rather than slopping around, which does not build up anything however long you do it, but instead tends to bore your horse and encourage him to be naughty!

Interval training may be used by many people, especially in the United States, and should be started during that last six weeks' build-up to the event if you have not started it before. Discuss with your trainer how much work you should be doing, with times and speeds being gradually increased as appropriate.

Do not make the mistake of wearing your horse out with work before you actually get to the competition. So often it is obvious that the horse has been worked into the ground before arrival by those desperate to ensure that their horses are fit enough. In their misguided efforts they have poured too much training and fitness work into the last ten days, when training should have eased up. The last gallop is usually best given between seven and ten days before the event, and a short sharp pipe-opener between five and seven days before the cross-country day. Apart from this the horse should just have been hacked out and kept sensible with some dressage, plus a couple of jumps to keep him alert.

On the other hand it is most important that your horse is fit enough for what you are expecting him to do. Make sure you have remembered to increase the quality of his food as the demands on him increase. This does not necessarily mean volume but at some stage the proportions of the mix you give him, or the amounts of protein and energy-giving foods, should be increased.

To remind you: oats, barley and sugar beet pulp are the main protein and energy-giving foods, with peas and beans also being very rich in protein. These last two are generally found in mixes but tend to be a bit heating and should be fed with discretion if they affect your horse in this way. A good supplement to make up any shortcoming in the diet should be included for the three-day event horse. Good quality hay is essential for the event horse and it is vital that you have the very best when he is competing. If you use haylage or other vacuum-packed varieties make sure you have your horse on this and used to it well before the event.

Many people take blood tests to help assess their horses' fitness. While not being infallible these can be a useful guide, but it is essential to take them at the same time of day and before the horse has worked in order to get a true picture. If one is taken before the horse has worked and the next is taken after you may get a wildly different reading. Take the first one about eight weeks before your three-day event and the second a month later. Taking one is no good as you will have no base with which to compare. Your vet will then discuss the results with you so that a decision can be made on the type of work and food which may be needed at this stage.

Think ahead about your worming programme so that your horse has this done not more than three or four weeks before the event, preferably over a quiet few days. Shoeing time is another point that needs careful working out. You do not want a new set put on the day before you travel but about seven to ten days before your horse is due on the cross-country. Your farrier will have to be told of your aims in plenty of time, and do not forget to ask him to make up at least one spare set to take with you.

Check your tack over carefully to make sure that everything is safe and in good condition. Look at your competition boots, if used, to ensure that they are safe and effective. If you need a new set it is best to use the boots a couple of times to wear them in a bit, as new ones can be slightly stiff and liable to rub a little until they have softened. Oil them well if appropriate.

It is even more important to go through all the kit, tack and general equipment (and what a lot it all seems) before packing up to stay away over a three-day event. The same principles apply as for a one-day event, but you will have to allow enough food for the duration of the competition. Make a list and divide it into sections to cater for the different phases and for the general bits and pieces, and tick it all off as you put it ready to be packed into the lorry or gooseneck. If it is a hot or long journey make sure that you take enough water and that you have the water, a bucket and if necessary a small feed easily accessible.

Try not to get your horse overexcited by all the preparations. Keep to your normal routine with him, but he may need his bath the day before you leave so perhaps a good time for this is on return from exercise. Any trimming can have been done during the previous couple of days. If the weather is changeable or cold be very careful not to let him catch a chill. If you are in any doubt, just wash mane, tail and legs but leave his body. This should be clean anyway if he has been conscientiously groomed!

COMPETITION INFORMATION

Following entry it is usual that you will be sent relevant information by the trials secretary, telling you the arrangements for the competition. This should include the time for the briefing and official tour of the roads and tracks, the vet check times and stabling arrangements, so once you have seen this you will be able to plan when and by which route to travel.

Although it seems a long time to be away, it is worth getting to the event in plenty of time in order to get organised and allow your horse to settle. The briefing and walk round can be a long affair and will not give you much time to ride afterwards, especially if the first veterinary inspection is that afternoon. So, unless you can ride early that day, you will find it will definitely make sense to arrive the day before and allow your horse to settle.

Generally three-day events are held over a weekend with Thursday as well as Friday being dressage days if it is a big competiton. The cross-country is on Saturday and show jumping on Sunday. This means that the briefing and vet's inspection are held on the Wednesday or Thursday, so you will need to plan to arrive on the Tuesday or Wednesday. To be confusing, however, quite a lot of events – especially on the continent – do the cross-country on Sunday and show jumping on Monday!

Just before the event you should receive a detailed programme for the whole competition and, possibly, a copy of the entries. This can be particularly useful for those hoping to share transport. You may, however, not receive this until you arrive for the briefing when you will be given a map of the course, roads and tracks, and general layout of the competition area. You should also receive your numbers. There are often different ones for dressage and show jumping and you must check to see if it is compulsory for your horse to wear his number whenever he is out of the stable. This is obligatory under FEI rules.

Study the event timetable carefully before you leave to ensure that you know basically what is going on. There are often all sorts of social functions, barbecues, competitions and grooms' parties etc. If you are camping at the event remember to have enough gear with you to cope with unexpected weather conditions. Changes of clothes and footwear seem to be never-ending at three-day events!

Make sure you have arranged to have a helper with you and if this person is not your usual groom at the event that he or she knows exactly what to expect and what to take or bring. It is essential to have someone with you at a three-day event to look after the horse generally and to help out on cross-country day. You will be far too busy walking courses, roads and tracks etc, as well as competing, to be able to look after your horse properly. If something ever went wrong it would be most unfair to the organisers of any event to be left to cope with any problems arising.

THE BRIEFING AND TOUR

It is essential that you, and your helper if possible, get to this to hear how everything is to be run, what you are or are not allowed to do, and to ask any questions about fences or other subjects. Do not be shy of asking; this is your chance to find out everything, and it is better to know now than make a mistake on the day.

After the briefing there is usually a mad rush to get into the front of a reasonably comfortable vehicle. If you are not using your own, try your best to get into someone else's in the front so that you can properly study where you are going. It is most important to take the map and a pen with you, so that you can tick off kilometre marks and any compulsory turning flags. If it is your first event it can all be a bit confusing and you may worry that you will not find your way, but usually on the day it is very obvious so long as you remember to count each kilometre mark as you pass it and know where, or how many times, you need to go through turning flags.

At some events it is difficult to do a second drive around the roads and tracks but usually (not always) the organisers do not mind you riding the route so long as you do not get close to any of the fences. This is, after all, only a test for the endurance side of the event and so many riders ride phase A one day and phase C the next, which certainly helps you get to know your way. Always check that you are

Horse and rider over a steeplechase fence met on phase B of the three-day event. This rider is a little far forward with the upper part of her body but is 'supporting' well with the hand. She is, however, riding too long through the stirrup, and as a result her leg has slipped back, offering little security should she need it. Steeplechase fences such as this one are common; some have ditches in front

allowed to ride round before setting off and if there are any restrictions on where you can ride. Look out for a suitable spot to do a short sharp canter, if possible, before getting to the steeplechase in order to prepare the horse for his next task.

At phase B everyone gets out of the vehicles to walk round. The course is usually two circuits or a figure-of-eight. The most important things to study are the approaches to your fences, the turns or corners and how sharp they are for a galloping horse, especially yours, and how much control you feel you will have. Look at the fences and think of how you must ride on into them and yet keep a firm hold to support your horse at speed.

Look very carefully at your channel through the finish to set off on your second circuit. This can look confusing on some courses, whereas on others it is very obvious. Remember you will be travelling fast so, once you do know where you are going, walk back 45m (50yds) or so to make sure it will look obvious when you are galloping.

About 300m after the finish of phase B there should be a checkover area, which is the only point on phase C where you may receive any assistance. Therefore you should have your helper here to ensure that you have still got all four shoes in place – if not, this is where the problem can be dealt with and, if it is very hot and you want to refresh your horse with a quick washdown, you can do so. Most people just get a quick checkover and carry on in walk rather than fuss the horse at this stage.

Another scramble back into vans, and phase C gets studied. Always look at the ground so that you know where you are going to have to go slowly, and where you can canter on a bit to make up time. You want to bring your horse in as quiet and relaxed as possible to the 10 minute halt, so that last half kilometre will need to be done almost at a walk or slow trot.

At the end of phase C everyone once again gets out for a walk after being shown the 10 minute 'box'. Look to see where everything is positioned and whether there is water laid on, as it is here that you will be bringing all your kit to refresh your horse during the break. Look out for a good place to put your bits and pieces, close to water, the 'loo' etc, and make a point of getting down early by putting some of your kit there to grab it on cross–country day. See how you get from the 'box' to the starting box to begin the cross-country, then where you finish and where the tent is for weighing at the end of the cross-country.

You are then left to walk the cross-country course and personally I feel very strongly that you should do this on your own, to assess your initial reaction to the fences. This, after all, will give you some idea of what your horse may also feel as he approaches the obstacles. Your first walk round should not be the one to decide how to jump the fences, but just to get an overall impression and know what you have to jump. Look at the ground and the lie of the land, learn where any turning flags are, and generally get a feel of the course. Your next walk is the serious one, which should be done with your trainer and when you really decide how each fence is going to be tackled. Your final walk should again be done alone so that you can plan clearly in your mind exactly how you intend to approach and jump each fence, and what alternative strategy you will employ should plan A not work for any reason.

THE FIRST HORSE INSPECTION

The first horse inspection indicates the official start of the event and every horse has to be passed by a panel, which includes a vet, before being allowed to start in the competition. For this your horse should be presented in a bridle, looking immaculate. In Britain the horses are always plaited but in other countries this may be so only at the top level. Check with other competitors but it looks professional to be plaited, if it does not overexcite the horse.

You should have practised running your horse up in hand at home. The important point to remember is to keep the horse's head straight at all times. If you do not, and his head is pulled round, he may well appear to nod and look lame. Carry a stick in case the horse misbehaves. The atmosphere at the vet's inspection can be intense, with so many horses milling around waiting for their turn, and therefore it is necessary to keep your wits about you – both so that your horse is safe from others, and that you do not miss your turn.

The first veterinary inspection in front of Badminton House – always a nerve-racking moment for all competitors. We can see that this horse is bent to the left, which may cause him to take irregular steps, making him appear not quite sound. It is very important to keep the horse straight whilst trotting in hand, and this should be practised at home

Make sure you are neatly turned out yourself, with sensible shoes in which to run up the horse. Keep him walking around and have a short practice before you go up for your turn in order to remind him what he is to do. Stand in front of him with both hands holding the rein either side of the bit whilst the panel have a look. Then walk straight away from them and trot on when required. Remember to turn your horse carefully and slowly away from you. This is when he could get a little excited and easily knock himself, so take your time and keep him under control.

Always pick out the feet before running the horse up, just in case a small stone has got lodged in the foot which could cause lameness. There have been several hard-luck stories of occasions when horses have been found to trot up lame for those vital few minutes. Keep away from other horses that are liable to kick out, and avoid rough or slippery ground.

THE DRESSAGE

You will have been given your start times soon after the vet's inspection is over, and so can plan how best to prepare for the dressage. With your knowledge of how your horse behaves in a one-day event you can work out a similar strategy to your normal one, but as your horse will be that much fitter and will be unaccustomed to this new style of competition it is best to allow for a little more work beforehand. There is considerably more atmosphere in a three-day event, which may well cause your 'fitter than ever' horse to overreact, so be prepared to cope with a rather more excitable or tense horse than usual.

Rather than riding your horse for hours all in one go, you are usually better off taking him out two or three times for an hour at a time. He will start to relax and get bored by 'yet another session' and in this way, although you will be working him hard, it will not overdo him before his cross-country. It may be best to wander about to look at the sights quietly on your first and/or last ride out before the test, or to get down and work the horse as soon as you have loosened him up. Remember that you may have to be a little more patient than usual, but quietly insist that your horse does eventually knuckle down and work properly. Avoid an argument if he is being a bit unco-operative, and keep changing the exercises until you achieve what you want. Your basic movements are the ones to start with, gradually increasing the impulsion and concentrating on rhythm and straightness.

American Bruce Davidson, former World Champion, shows elegant style during his test on Dr Peaches in Seoul. Notice how three of the horse's feet are flat on the ground during this canter movement. The top hat, tailed coat, white breeches and top boots, with gloves and spurs, are correct dress for dressage in advanced competition

Avoid having to do too much to the horse at the last minute. Plan ahead about when the horse should be plaited. It is best to get this done in plenty of time, in case you feel you need to stay out riding the horse until the last minute. If you intend to use studs, put them in early. Have your tack clean and ready beforehand with your number already attached to your competition bridle. Warm up in brushing boots, but have an easily removable set so that you are not going to have to stand for long while these are taken off.

Make sure you are correctly dressed with everything clean, neat and tidy. The hair should be in a bun if a top hat is worn. This should be absolutely straight and worn horizontal to the ground. Boots should

lished, and spurs worn correctly with the shank, if curved,
 ʒ downwards. Gloves, if worn, should be of a light colour. In
 ' or FEI tests gloves and spurs are compulsory.
 ır horse moving before his test and do not stand around.
 ɔots removed in plenty of time before going in, and
 rough your test. Do not go into the arena with your
 ry to get trotting or cantering round your arena at the
 ꜰꜱ. ɔpportunity, so that your horse can see the judges' boxes and
get used to any arena decorations. Listen for the bell, take a few deep
breaths, and work on getting a good entrance and doing the best test of
which you are capable.

Afterwards it may be sensible to put boots back on to return to the
stables, in case your horse plays up.

The pipe-opener

Whether your dressage is the day before the cross-country or two days
before, your horse should have a short, sharp pipe-opener to clear his
wind the day before his cross-country. This is generally done after his
dressage. Do not take any risks. Put on your galloping kit and find a
suitable spot to do a couple of short sharp bursts. Allow your horse to
walk until he is cool before bringing him back to the stables. His hay
should be reduced to half his normal amount the night before he goes
cross-country.

CROSS-COUNTRY DAY

Your horse's normal feeding time may well have to be adjusted to suit
your times for the day. He should be given a smallish feed 4–6 hours
before he is due to run, and then no more food until he has finished.
Water should be freely available up until 2 hours before he runs. In
extreme heat offer water up until 1 hour before.

Electrolytes can be added to the water if your horse is accustomed to
them, but do not do this if you have not used them in this way before
as it may put the horse off altogether. If possible leave your horse to
rest as long as possible, and avoid fussing him. You will need to put
your studs in and make a top plait to which you can tie the bridle with a
shoelace, or something similar and strong. Have your tack ready and
waiting to be put on, having weighed it and yourself in plenty of time
and adjusted the weight in your weight cloth if necessary. Have your
spurs, number, stick and hat ready to be put on.

Earlier you or your helper will have ensured that you have taken the main necessities to 'the box'. This should include washing-down kit, grease for the cross-country, coolers, sweat rugs, and blankets as necessary, spare set of shoes and studs, spare leathers, irons, bridle, boots, overreach (bell) boots, towels, waterproofs, first-aid kit, spare stick and gloves, coat, drink, glucose tablets, a spare set of timings, etc. Remember to do your horse justice by having breakfast before what is a fairly strenuous day. Your body requires a little more than black coffee if it is to cope effectively, so start the day by giving it some sustenance on which to keep going!

Work out how long you need to get to the start of phase A, and arrive there about 10 minutes before you are due away – longer, if you are tacking up and weighing out there. Bring enough lead with you to ensure that you have enough to make the compulsory minimum weight of 75kg (165lb). As phase A is the warm-up it is unnecessary to do any more work before setting off. Check your watch against the official time, set this, and make sure your stopwatch is rewound.

Times and watches
It is essential that you are aware of the importance of times in a three-day event, as time penalties are very costly. Your times are worked out from an optimum time for each phase, with each being quite independent of the other. Loss of time in one cannot therefore be compensated by gain of time in another. Phases A and C, the roads and tracks, are normally carried out at a speed of 200–220m per minute, which works out at a steady trot or canter. The speeplechase speed will vary between approximately 600 and 690m per minute and the cross-country from approximately 500 to 570m per minute. The actual speed depends on the standard of the competition.

However, when given your times for the competition they will show your scheduled start and finish times for each phase. Personally I recommend that you disregard your actual starting time and work from a twelve o'clock start, which means your stopwatch – if you have one – and ordinary watch will basically work on the same time. Should there be any kind of hold-up in the competition, which can and does happen, this need not then affect you because all you do, when told you have 5 minutes before you start, is set your watch at five to twelve. Using your real time means that if there is any delay all your times are completely wrong!

Most competitors work out their times for the roads and tracks allowing a basic 4 minutes per kilometre. This works out about right, giving a little in hand at the start of phase B which is necessary for checking girths and shortening stirrups, if you have not already done so on the way in from phase A. Your first kilometre will probably take 5 minutes as you will bring your horse back to a walk after finishing the steeplechase, and will not want to rush the recovery time. But be careful not to get more than a minute behind, as it will become quite difficult to catch up. Ideally, you want to come in from phase C a couple of minutes early to give you just that little bit of extra time in the 10 minute box.

It is very important not to be late into the 10 minute box so keep up to time and, when it comes to getting ready for phase D, the cross-country, you should be on your horse walking him up at least 1½ minutes before you are due to start. You should be hovering around the start box by 15 seconds before your time to go. In your first three-day event it is better to be a little early for everything, until you know what to expect, than get in a panic and not do things such as checking girths etc properly because you have left everything a bit late.

Ten-minute halt

Ask an experienced rider to check your times and run over your programme of how you intend to work in the vet box – it will be helpful and maybe give you an idea or two on how to improve on your plans. Watch how others do everything and remember the secret is to rest and refresh your horse, not hurry and hassle it.

When you come towards the vet box you will usually have been told to trot steadily straight towards the inspection panel for 45m (50yd) or so, and through the finish of phase C. Keep going until you have done this, before dismounting when the panel tell you. They will look at the horse and probably check his heart rate and breathing. They may ask to see you again in 5 minutes if either of the readings are high, in order to ensure these are settling all right after a rest period. If it is not too hot let the horse walk quietly, having loosened girths and noseband. Put a wet sponge in his mouth to refresh him, and sponge him down well as necessary, quickly and quietly, without getting water over his back which could cause muscle spasm. Keep him walking with a sweat rug or cooler or whatever on, according to the weather.

If it is very hot the use of ice to cool the main blood vessels, and iced towels placed over the poll behind the ears, are beneficial if used with discretion. Washing down, scraping and washing down again help to cool the horse, but if it is your first time fitting all this in might not be a success unless you have an experienced helper to ensure everything is being done in the best interests of the horse and to keep you aware of time.

159

For the rider's benefit, make use of the loo; if necessary have a small drink; and discuss what fences, if any, are causing trouble so that you can decide whether plan A or B seems to make more sense. Have a clean pair of gloves ready, reset your watch once you know when you should be on, and check girths are tightened as you get on. If you use grease get your helper to put this down over stifles and joints last, and make sure she does not put greasy hands anywhere near your reins! Get down near the start box and wake your horse up so that he is alert and ready for the most exciting part of all – the cross-country.

Weighing-in
At the end of your round pull your horse up gradually and bring him back to the weighing-in tent before dismounting in front of the official steward. Do not leap off your horse in any other place, under penalty of elimination. Unsaddle the horse without letting anyone other than the official steward near until you have been weighed and signed the weight sheet.

Aftercare
As soon as you have weighed in the trials vets may well have a quick look at your horse, and he now needs to be kept walking quietly until he stops blowing. Whether to wash him down or not at this stage rather depends on the weather, but generally the most important thing is to let the horse's breathing and heart rate return to normal as soon as possible. A quick look over will have told you whether there are any obvious injuries which might need attention and, if so, the vet should be notified. Otherwise quietly walk the horse back to the stables for general attention.

A thorough wash down, with a body wash if preferred and soap on the legs to help remove the grease, will refresh and cool the horse. Do not let him stand longer than absolutely necessary but take him for a walk again until he dries off, his breathing and heart rate have returned completely to normal, and he is ready to have some hay. During this time short drinks, with electrolytes if he is used to them, can have been offered so long as his breathing is more or less normal.

Once your horse is comfortable put on day bandages, kaolin or your own leg-care favourite, and leave him to rest for a few hours. Keep an eye on him to ensure that he is warm enough but not getting too hot. Sometimes horses break out in a cold sweat at this time, and he may need another walk and his ears gently massaged. If these are cold the horse will not be comfortable. A small feed should be given, with salt or electrolytes when suitable, and another small one later. After a strenuous day he will not want to be confronted with an enormous feed.

Take your horse out for a short walk before it gets too late and trot him up to see that all is well. If it is, then reset his rugs and leave him in peace to settle for the night. If you are worried or there is the slightest sign of a problem, call the competition vet who will advise you. Do not give anything yourself as you may end up contravening the drug rules. The vet is there to help you and advise on this sort of problem, and will do his best to get your horse right for the final day.

THE FINAL INSPECTION

This is the most important one of all as the jury has to decide whether the horses are fit enough to continue in the competition. Of course the majority are fine, but there are always one or two who may trot up looking a bit stiff and sore and the jury must decide whether it is in the best interests of these horses to be allowed to do that one round of show jumps or not, as further work may aggravate the problem.

Presentation is everything at this time. Get up early to see your horse, walk him out for 5 or 10 minutes to unstiffen him, then see him trot up. Look carefully to ensure that he is level. If all is well, take him back and give him his breakfast. If things do not look good, try walking for another 10 minutes and see if he gets better. If things still do not look good, or there is an obvious hot spot or swelling on the legs, call the vet immediately and be guided by his judgement and follow his advice.

Plait your horse, wash off any poultice and tidy him up, and then take him for a quiet hack for 20 minutes to loosen him up thoroughly so that you return ready for the vet's inspection. Keep him walking so that he does not stiffen up again. This is very important. Then present him in front of the panel as you did at the first inspection.

THE SHOW JUMPING

This final phase is difficult not because of the size of the fences, but because the horse has covered a long and tiring course over solid fences the day before. How this has affected him will be difficult to tell until you are actually in the arena, but the warming up beforehand plays an important part.

Show jumping is the last discipline of the three-day event, and this part of the competition can be extremely difficult when riding a horse which is tired after the cross-country phase the previous day. This horse seems to have a good outlook and is jumping in a nice style, and is neat in front. The rider is leaning slightly to the right, which could interfere with the horse's balance

First walk your course carefully. Usually this must be done properly dressed, after a certain time and always under FEI rules. Check when the course is open and when you can walk before looking to decide your route. The speeds are usually faster than at one-day trials so you must look extra carefully to decide where you can safely save time by, for example, cutting inside a fence.

Loosen your horse up slowly and carefully – he will probably have stiffened up again since the final inspection, and will need a bit of time to get going again. The secret on the third day is to loosen your horse up sufficiently without tiring him. It is better to do some suppling work on the flat for 10 minutes than to jump him too often. When you feel he is ready – and you may well have to wake him up – pop him over a cross-pole once or twice, a vertical, and then do a couple of jumps over a good spread to ensure he is 'opening up' well.

In three-day events it is usual to jump in reverse order of merit after the speed and endurance, but do not forget there may have been one or two drop-outs overnight so be ready to jump on time. It can be most exciting watching how the placings change during this phase. A clear round may move you up several places and certainly ensures that you stay where you are.

After your round keep your horse warm, as it is usual for all finishers to go in for the final prize-giving. This is the highlight of riding in a three-day event, whether you finish first or in the back row, because it is a tremendous achievement to finish all three days on the same horse knowing that you have between you come through to complete such a true all-round test of horse and rider.

AFTER IT IS ALL OVER

The care of your horse after a three-day event is vital to future success. After you have finished you may pack up straight away or wait until the next day to start the journey home, but in the excitement do not forget that your horse will need special attention at this time to help him relax mentally, and remember to give the best care to his legs and to watch how they react. A slight strain may not be obvious for a day or two, so keep a special look-out each morning for any heat or swelling and treat as necessary.

If your horse is the type that gallops about in the field you would be best hacking him out quietly, and leading him out to graze, until he is sufficiently relaxed and settled to be sensible out on his holiday – which every horse deserves following a three-day event. How long this should be depends on the horse, how the event went, what your future plans are, the stage of the season, severity of the course and what would be best for your horse. Either way, three weeks is the minimum break the horse should have, whatever the standard of the course. Three-day events generally tend to round off a season, so you will usually have done a fair few events by now and this is the time to let the horse down for a good long break or a shorter one. Then keep time ticking over to build up experience and make further improvements before tackling another three-day event the following season.

After your three-day event take a look back at the season and decide where things could be improved. Assess whether your horse is capable and seems confident to aim a little higher. Study any video film or photographs, and see if these indicate anything which might need to be improved so that you can work on it for the next season. How your horse comes out of the competition will tell you a lot about your fitness programme and whether he was having the right amount of food. If he looks and feels generally good then things must have gone well – this is how it should be. If the horse looks generally tired and listless afterwards, a blood test should be taken to see if he needs any veterinary help, and you must evaluate the position and discuss how to improve your horse's fitness and feeding programme ready for the next time.

A three-day event will tell you a lot about your horse, but it may not be until the next competition that you will know for sure that he was as happy and confident about it all as you think. It is always wise to treat your next outing with caution and keep it small, just in case your horse has in fact had a bit of fright. It only happens to a few horses, but it is sensible to play safe.

The opposite happened with Warrior – he was so cock-a-hoop after winning Burghley (only his second three-day event) that he ran away with me at the next event. He ran out at two fences because I was unable to control him, and he then tipped me off at the water before disappearing – horses are great levellers!

CHAPTER 9

Coping with Common Problems

This chapter deals with the little problems which occur inevitably and frequently along the road to success. They have to be overcome, cured and learnt from, whether they be mental, physical or unavoidable. There are horses which despite initial promise simply fail to progress; others do not have the necessary courage when the chips are down. Brilliant horses may appear which do not have the legs to cope with the demands of the sport. Temperament plays a big part too, and sometimes a temperamental horse in the wrong hands can become lethal when fit to run at three-day level, but be brilliant with the right rider. Unexpected problems such as a nail through a foot the day before the event, the horse with colic, the lorry that breaks down making you fail to reach the competition in time – you name it, it can and has happened to anyone and everyone at sometime or other. The following may give some helpful advice on coping with or helping to prevent some of the more common problems.

ASKING TOO MUCH TOO SOON

This is probably the most common of all and problems resulting from this may present themselves in numerous different ways. A young horse will only be able to take so much work, according to his experience and physical ability at that stage, and the vital thing to remember here is when to stop. A promising horse can go brilliantly in three or four events and one is tempted to go to just one event too many. Something happens, such as a bad fall or a refusal, which in itself may seem nothing because the horse then continued on round the course all right. But this must be taken as a warning.

Why did the horse fall? Going too fast and getting over-confident? In this case a fall can teach him a lesson and make him a better horse. Was it, however, your position over the fence or coming into it which resulted in the horse being pushed into a situation with which he simply could not cope – had you pushed him so far onto his forehand

These two seem to be having fun in a pairs' cross-country competition. These competitions are very useful for encouraging younger horses round a course with an older, more experienced colleague as a guide. The rider in front is preparing herself for rather a sticky landing, as her horse took off a bit too early. She is sitting back slightly but giving the horse the essential freedom of his head and neck. The second horse was a little more deliberate about his jump

---

One of the feature fences at the Gatcombe Horse Trials is the 'big steps', which can be jumped either up or down hill. It is very important to keep balanced and the horse well **in** hand when coming down the steps, as shown here, and to keep driving him forward to maintain the momentum to the top when going up them

as you approached that he could not get himself together to clear the fence? This situation can be really unnerving to the young horse who has built up trust and confidence in you, tries his hardest despite you, and then ends up in a heap on the ground. All very frightening, and the start of the downhill road unless you can quickly sort out what went wrong and put it right so that it never happens again.

Refusals may happen because the horse was being overfaced. Sometimes the courses are not as straightforward as you had been led to believe, and you arrive to find your so-called straightforward course far more imposing than expected but decide to have a go anyway. A very experienced rider can ride a green horse and give him confidence by being very positive and making the best of the course by choosing the easiest options everywhere. Such a rider can turn this problem into an advantage because the horse builds up confidence as him goes along and so finishes feeling very pleased with himself.

With a novice or inexperienced rider this is unlikely to be the case, and both horse and rider set off feeling unsure of what to expect. This lack of positive thinking is hopeless once one side or the other meets something with which it does not know how to cope, and so a refusal results. Half-hearted efforts to get the horse over usually result in failure as the rider honestly does not know how to approach the problem. At this point the horse has realised that if he stops he gets away from the problem, as after a couple of further tries he goes home and the rider becomes demoralised through apparent failure.

If you cannot ride positively enough round the courses and something goes wrong which you cannot cope with at the time through strong riding and firm use of the stick, you are generally best to retire and ask if you can go back afterwards to sort out the problem

---

Ireland's Melanie Duff and Clarence II show the way round Burghley in 1987. Note the grease on the horse's forearms and down over its knees, as well as down the front of the hindlegs. This helps prevent the horse from injuring itself should it straddle or get tied up in a fence. The grease will help the horse 'glide off' the hazard, without tearing the skin too much, and is usually very effective in preventing further injury

INSET: *David O'Connor (USA) and Border Raider sail over this wide obstacle at Burghley in 1987. Notice how the horse is really lifting his forelegs, as he has obviously stood off some way from the fence, and is having to really use himself to clear it. A good event horse will help its rider out in this way*

A confident enough jump by this young horse, but the rider is allowing her lower leg to slide back too much so that her weight is too far forward, instead of being down into the heel. Maintaining a good leg position is very important, especially as the fences get bigger

with your helper. You should then go off for further cross-country schooling at a place where you can find a similar situation, and work out the problem and teach the horse to master the technique of this particular type of fence. Very often the problem has arisen because you have approached at the wrong speed, perhaps too fast for a combination or with not enough impulsion for a spread. You may also have confused the horse by not allowing him to see a way out clearly enough.

Your position can make a lot of difference, as we have already mentioned, and it may be that this plus your speed is hindering the horse especially if you are also not using enough leg into your fences. Sit up well, keep hold of your horse to support him on the approach, and keep your leg on throughout the jump.

FALLS

One fall can be the result of overconfidence or inexperience, or perhaps because of the ground conditions.

Frequent falls usually occur because the rider has got too far forward and is in front of the horse's centre of gravity over the fences. The rider may be using too much sudden movement of his body in the air, which also contributes towards unbalancing the horse.

Riding on too loose a rein is another contributing factor. With the extra speed the horse does need supporting for the landing stride, so that he will not 'peck' and pitch a loose rider over his ears!

If the horse is a careless jumper he will need holding together well throughout the course, and this sort of horse may well be prone to falls if he does not try too hard or fails to respect solid fences. It may be that he is too tense or tight in his jumping to use himself properly, and so needs to be taught to take things more in his stride and to relax more. Steady cantering over endless jumps until he starts to concentrate and use himself over the fences may be the answer. If this works you may need to give him quite a bit of work before setting off round the cross-country.

Some horses require a strong leg aid on the take-off stride, others are better if you sit still. But if your various efforts fail and you continue to end up on the floor, it may be time to consider another rider for that horse or even a different sport altogether. Not every horse is necessarily going to make a good eventer and one that falls too often, no matter whose fault it is, will be unlikely to make the top, as a good horse will normally end up taking over and either look after itself, or stop going for that particular rider.

HORSES THAT DISLIKE WATER

This is not an uncommon problem but one which it is essential to overcome early, as the very nature of the sport ensures that most courses have a water jump of some sort. If the horse is just starting it is most important that you make a serious effort to get into, over and through every stream, puddle, etc, that you can find, so that he is quite used to it all from the word go. It is so essential that your horse is confident about water in general before ever he has to tackle it in competition. Very often problems are caused by horses never being given the chance to sort out the basic principles before meeting a proper water jump in competition.

When introducing a horse to water it is very important that the bottom is firm and will not 'give' underneath the horse's weight. Allow the horse to familiarise himself with the strange noise, and shiny surface, before asking him to enter; remember to be firm but kind. From early on in training it is important that the horse learns not to run away from things which frighten him

(right) *A beautifully straight jump into the lake at Badminton by Olympic Champion Mark Todd. Straightness and a controlled approach make all the difference when riding into water. Maintaining balance on landing and focussing on any obstacle to be jumped on the way out then take priority*

Just splashing through the odd river or stream is hardly proper preparation for a big log over a drop into water, but it is a start. Your thinking horse is bound to be surprised and confused if confronted with something that requires a certain technique which he has not mastered before. So spend time getting the horse used to jumping in and out of water over a drop, then over a log or fence into the water. Then make sure he jumps a fence actually in the water. He should be totally confident about doing this long before he meets anything like it in competition.

Make sure your approach is not too fast but has enough impulsion to get into the water safely. Be very firm and positive, not just on the approach but also on those last few strides before take-off. Do not stop riding until the horse is airborne.

If the horse is treated in this way and is ridden correctly, water should not cause a problem. The rider, however, must remember to sit up well on landing to balance the horse before the next stride. This is so often when the horse will stumble and fall as the drag of the water catches him, if the rider is not in a safe, upright position on landing.

THE OVERSTRONG HORSE

Control is of paramount importance and it is nothing short of suicidal to be galloping over big solid obstacles without having the horse under control. A confident and fully fit horse can be very different from the raw novice doing his first few events, so the snaffle bridle used then may be totally inappropriate now.

It is not always easy to decide on the right bit, as we have already discussed, but if your horse is getting too strong you must do something before an accident occurs. There are more and more bits with which to experiment appearing on the market, and do not forget that martingales and nosebands used in conjunction with a different bit can make a big difference.

All too often a horse becomes very strong because the rider is not using a powerful enough leg to push it up into the bridle and off its forehand, but is just pulling on its mouth so the horse pulls back. The 'You pull at me and I will pull at you' syndrome does exist and a compromise must be reached. Choose a new bit which is difficult for the horse to lean on, such as one of the roller types or a simple gag, and if the horse opens his mouth a lot use a flash or grackle (crossover) noseband to prevent him.

Some horses are much easier in a three-day event when they have done a lot of the work round the steeplechase and roads and tracks, and therefore have settled and will listen more to the rider. They may, however, be very strong round the steeplechase. My own horse Warrior was very difficult in this way but I found that if I did the steeplechase in the roller gag I could then take the reins off the gag in the 10 minute halt, and put them on the rings, so that I did the cross-country with a roller snaffle. This was quite sufficient as Warrior respected the solid fences and always steadied himself before them – he did not do this over the birch steeplechase fences!

Some people change to a totally different bridle in the box, finding that one bit for the steeplechase and another for the cross-country works well. Remember however that the horse may be a little excited at this point, and not as easy to put a new bridle on as he is in his stable!

THE HORSE THAT REARS AT THE START

Watching the cross-country start is quite an enlightening experience as the reaction of the rider at this point of the competition is clearly evident in the behaviour of the horse.

Of course it is an exciting moment as you finally get into the start box ready for the off. Your adrenalin is flowing well, the horse is on its toes and the feeling of anticipation is intense. It therefore does not take very much for the horse, being restricted in a small space and not allowed to go forward, to release his pent-up energy upwards in a rear or a series of rears and leaps!

Calmness on the part of the rider plays a very big part and this must extend down to the hands on the reins, which must remain soft. Do NOT get into the start box a moment before you need, if your horse is highly strung. Keep him moving forwards, round in a circle if possible, having at some stage gone into and out of the box so that you know, when the count down starts, he will in fact go in as required. Some horses will be quite happy facing backwards and may stand for a short time looking out this way, but cannot take looking forwards. Keep calm and keep moving if you have this problem and it will rarely get too serious. If you cannot get into the box have a calm competent helper to lead you in, but they must again be soft with the hand on the rein. The slightest pull down on the mouth and the horse will tend to go up.

Tell the starter if your horse is apt to be difficult and how you intend to cope, so that he will not hassle you about getting into the start box too soon. Keep calm and keep walking forward so that the horse's

175

frustrations are kept on an even keel going forwards rather than up, sideways or backwards.

NAPPING

The same sort of problem can arise when trying to enter the show jumping arena. This may be made worse if you have been sitting around for some time in the collecting ring. The horse does not want to leave the security of this and go out into the arena. A simple sharp reminder with the whip, whilst allowing the horse to go forward, is usually all that is required, with a strong positive leg thereafter. The more persistent horse may need leading in, even at the run at times.

It is, I am afraid, a reflection on the basic obedience training if this really becomes a problem. If your horse does not go forward when asked he is basically disobedient. You cannot allow this situation. Somewhere along the line he has been getting away with something, however small it may have seemed, and has started to question your authority. He may well be a bit worked up over the occasion and perhaps rear in excitement, but if he then refuses to go forwards when asked he is being plain nappy.

This can lead quite quickly to all sorts of horrors such as rushing backwards, fly jumps backwards or forwards, lashing out and uncontrollable charging off with the bit well between the teeth – all totally unacceptable! A nappy horse is basically a naughty one but you must ask yourself why this is happening, particularly if previously you have had no trouble. If you are on top it is difficult to see the horse's eye but this will tell you a lot, so ask your helper to watch his eye carefully when he plays up in order to get an idea from his expression.

If the horse has been suffering pain from somewhere it will be accentuated in a competitive atmosphere. A back strain or pulled muscle may not be obvious at home when you ride him for shorter periods, but may be aching quite a lot by the time the horse has travelled for hours to an event, then been worked hard, put away, stiffened up, worked again etc, and he might well be wondering whether it is all worth it from his point of view.

If his teeth have got very sharp and you are not the world's most sensitive rider and catch him in the mouth a few times, especially when you are a bit nervous in the competitive atmosphere, you should well understand what a turn–off that might be. Look in his mouth: has he torn the sensitive corners of his mouth, or does he look sore anywhere there?

Could he be jarred by the hard ground, making him sore either in feet or legs or further up in his shoulders? No horse is going to want to continue jumping in these conditions if he is suffering before he even gets to the competition. If his behaviour is out of character then very often a good break to let nature heal is the best way, after the vets have had a good look to see that nothing more serious is wrong or that his back is not the problem. A tough sport like eventing inevitably causes a few problems here, particularly if you have had a fall at any stage.

On the other hand, if you have checked and discounted all these things you could be dealing with a very naughty horse who requires strong riding, a good deal of discipline, and hours of work to get to the bottom of him so that he is obedient. The time is spent making sure that he never gets away with the slightest thing. It can be disheartening but perseverance is the key.

My own two superstars were both extremely difficult. My little Olympic horse 'Our Nobby' was so nappy that I was not allowed to

This photograph shows Warrior, former winner of Badminton and Burghley, and member of World and European teams. He is now enjoying his retirement from three-day eventing, and is seen here in the field with one of the up-and-coming stars of tomorrow. Horses turned away to pasture should be checked at least once a day

ride him for three months until my brother and sister felt he was safe, and it once took us 5 hours to persuade him to jump the ditch part of a coffin because he was so obstinate and bolshy. Once he realised he was not going to get away with it he settled down to become a brilliant performer, going from Pony Club team to a Badminton win and on to an Olympic Team Gold Medal. He was only 15hh and very nearly defied all our efforts, but he had the ability and luckily my family had the patience – I cannot claim that mine as a teenager was always quite so good!

Warrior was totally different and a real thinker who would catch one out the whole time if you did not constantly do everything absolutely 100 per cent right. Luckily he is such a bighead that he would never let his audience down (if it was big enough) and always went brilliantly when it really mattered. To this day if you approach a fence wrong on him he will stop – it is one way of learning how to ride! He was more naughty than really nappy however.

THE HORSE THAT GETS TIRED

If the horse is properly trained, has been brought on consistently and has had enough work to be finding it easy at home, generally at one-day level he should be fit enough if he is ridden considerately round the course in competition.

There are several factors which will influence the horse's performance which you should consider if you find your horse gets excessively tired.

Firstly, is he getting the right amount of food for the work he is doing and for the type of horse he is? Is he getting enough energy-giving food and if so is the quality good? Bad food will do nothing for a horse. Increase his rations, check quality and see if he copes better at the next event. Does he look good in his coat, bright in his eye and well covered on his top line without in any way being too fat? Is his skin pliable and loose, and does he generally look alert, happy and well? If you are worried get the vet to check his heart and lungs and do a blood test. He may have been suffering from a slight virus which was not enough to show in itself but showed up in an event. Once you know the results of this you can follow your vet's advice.

Maybe you were not doing quite enough cantering, as this is the pace which builds up the lung capacity, bringing the diaphragm into use with the motion of the horse. Do not forget that the weather will play a big part as well as the course. A very tiring hilly course in very

This rider is sitting safely upright with an excellent firm leg position and is looking ahead for the next fence on her novice horse. The horse, however, looks on the fat side and would need to look considerably leaner before tackling more advanced and strenuous courses without endangering its wind and legs

hot and humid conditions can be extremely energy-sapping. Your style of riding in these conditions needs to be fairly sympathetic if you are to conserve enough of your horse's energy to cope with the last few fences without really doing the animal in.

If you have a young horse, or it is the first time the horse has really been made fit, you may need to just ride him steadily round the courses until he has a holiday. It is nearly always the case that they come up much better the second time and on subsequent occasions.

The breeding of your horse will also make a big difference in some cases. It is well proven that the thoroughbred or near-thoroughbred is the ideal event type as it has outstanding stamina. Many other crossbreds are now being aimed at eventing and, although a lot do very well, there are inevitably some who find the speed a bit much over such solid fences and for the distance required. The heavier type of horse will always be at a slight disadvantage, and the breeding of many warm bloods etc was never designed for speed but much more for dressage and jumping, at which they excell.

Check through all these factors when trying to assess why your horse feels tired on the course and see where improvements can be made. He will inevitably feel a bit tired near the end of the course at the beginning of the season, but this should improve as time goes on and as he sharpens up with each outing.

SPOOKY HORSES

These horses can be a real problem in all phases, but perhaps most particularly in the dressage. They may spook down the centre line, over the centre line, at every flower arrangement or marker decorating the arena, at the judge's car, and even at their own shadow. Jumping can also be a problem, with the horse taking fright at zig-zags, and spooking or jumping at sponsors' banners around the arena or on the cross–country course. There is no doubt about it, such things are a menace!

Basically, I am afraid, a spooky horse remains a spooky horse but generally they do improve with age and experience. You have to work them in well so that they are listening to you rather than noticing all the spooks around the place. Be positive and try to think shoulder-in away from the spooks, with a strong inside leg keeping the horse's head firmly looking away from the object to the inside.

Patience is a virtue with these horses as generally they get worse if you get after them, but after a period of time you will probably need to be a bit tough and get them to toe the line.

In a test these horses can be very difficult. Get round the arena as soon as you possibly can, circle the judge's car if you feel that may be a problem, and twist in and out of any markers or flowers making quite sure that the horse is sufficiently under control not to shoot away from an object and actually into the arena. Do not make an issue of anything but apply the same principle of using shoulder-in to keep the horse's head looking away from the problem. Keep as still as you can when crossing the centre line so that the horse does not break his stride if he spooks at the cross or something else. Whatever you do do not get frustrated, however annoying the situation might be.

In the jumping just be very careful not to get caught out, and be quick with your reactions. Be ready for him to spook away from something, when you must immediately compensate with strong legs and keep hold of the horse so that he cannot get too far off course.

THE TENSE HORSE

This is a slightly different problem which should be possible to alleviate quite considerably as the horse gets more confident and learns to relax. Initially, the more often the horse can be taken out and about the better, whether competing or not. Just to go out and work at a competition is a very good way of settling the horse. Lungeing is another excellent method of relaxing him without the weight of the rider. Side reins should be used to keep the horse under control and working correctly, but remember to have rests and loosen these every 15 minutes or so to encourage the horse to relax and stretch, and to avoid overtiring his muscles.

Sometimes it is best to use the little-and-often method. This means taking the horse out, either ridden or lunged, initially for half an hour and then putting it away. Take it out ridden next, work for another half hour and put it away. Then do this once again, so that the horse starts to get bored with the endless cycle and will be glad to concentrate more on the work and less on itself.

At other times walking about on a loose rein, watching the sights and sounds, can be all that is necessary. The horse simply needs the time to relax and, once it has got over the feeling of anticipation, will settle to work well. If this is the way to settle your horse remember to allow plenty of time on arrival.

The tense horse always needs time, and everything needs to be done in a quiet, calm way. On arrival sit for 5 minutes before opening everything up so that the sudden flurry of activity, inevitable on arrival, has a less exciting effect. Before each phase walk your horse for 10 minutes before doing anything else. Gradually over a period of time it will get less tense as it becomes more confident and experience takes over from anticipation.

BAD TRAVELLERS

One of the most difficult problems can be the bad traveller. There is nothing more frustrating than to arrive late because your horse has panicked, thrown itself around or, even worse, injured itself en route to the event. Quite apart from the poor horse, everyone arrives in a state and the whole day starts disastrously.

You will normally have some idea about how your horse travels before setting off to your event as you will have been around a bit anyway, but any problem may be less serious on short journeys. Some horses are all right in one horse box but not others, or will travel forwards or backwards but not herringbone, or vice-versa.

The most usual problem is that for one reason or another the horse feels insecure, especially on turns, so check how this could be improved. Metal floors, regardless of how much straw etc is on top, can still be very slippery. Thick rubber is one of the best surfaces to travel on as it is non-slip and absorbs jarring and jolting, but it is heavy and in hot weather can be quite heating. There are also various special so-called non-slip surfaces which can be applied to the floor. Many are quite good but some certainly become very slippery if the floor gets wet. Whatever you decide is best, remember that the horse must feel safe and secure.

The size of the partitioning can be the real answer to the problem. Unless the horse can spread his legs far enough apart to balance himself – and some require a lot more room for this than others – he will never really settle but lean against the walls and struggle to keep his legs. Very often the horse will prefer travelling backwards to forwards and will feel more secure like this than sideways, but either way so long as you increase the width they will usually improve greatly and, with more confidence, give up panicking, kicking etc altogether.

It helps to travel with a steady horse and a haynet may encourage the nervous animal to settle quicker. Keep the haynet small if you are to compete cross-country that day.

BAD LOADERS

This is definitely the worst of the lot! Try to overcome this problem at home before you want to go off anywhere.

You may simply need to practise every day luring the horse with food and leading him in and out with a little gentle encouragement from the stick or broom (an excellent way of pushing the slightly reluctant horse up the ramp!).

Far too often handlers are the real problem as they will pull on the horse's head too much, with the result that the animal throws his head up and hits the top of the box, making it even more reluctant. Keep the rein as slack as possible and the head down. If a little persuasion from the ground does not work get the lunge line attached to one side of the trailer or box, take the other round the back of the horse and apply firm pressure forward up the ramp. Ideally, if you have two helpers, get one to take a second rope or rein and cross over behind the horse, so that both helpers are pulling the horse forward up the ramp from behind with their lines.

Make sure you park in a suitable spot where the ramp sits at its least steep, and make sure that the ramp rests firmly and securely on the ground. Watch your horse's eye to ascertain whether it looks frightened, apprehensive, or just plain stubborn, and react accordingly. It will often help for the horse to see another one load, not just already in there. So if you anticipate trouble bring two out together, put one in, and hope yours will get the message! Allow plenty of time, be firm without getting cross and make sure you win the day in the end. Have your horse well protected with travelling gear suitable for the journey, especially if he is a bad traveller and liable to kick around, or you know he messes about before loading. Always reward the difficult loader when you get him there so that he learns it's worth his while in the end, despite what your own feelings are at the time!

CHAPTER 10

Helpful Hints

This final chapter is designed to give you extra useful information on various aspects of the sport which it will be necessary for you to know as you aim for either your first three-day event or work towards a higher standard. While national federations have adapted rules to suit local needs these are all based on those laid down by the FEI, and these include the following excerpts. I have also given some hints on common injuries which tend to crop up from time to time, and general advice on how to cope with or prevent them.

The following are excerpts from the present *Rules for Three-Day Events* which are particularly important to understand. It is vital that you know your own national rules covering these points; remember that national events will normally be run under your own national rules unless stated otherwise, whereas international events come under the jurisdiction of FEI rules.

CRUELTY
Any act or series of actions which, in the opinion of the Ground Jury, can clearly and without doubt be defined as cruelty, shall be penalised by elimination.

Such acts include: Excessive pressing of an exhausted horse.

Excessive use of whip and/or spurs.

Whips and spurs: Whips must not be weighted at the end or exceed 75cm (30 inches) in length. Spurs capable of wounding a horse are forbidden.

An official must be appointed to inspect whips and spurs before any Test. He has the authority to refuse permission for any competitor to start, whose whip or spurs contravene this Article. He will immediately report the circumstances to the Ground Jury for confirmation.

EXCESSIVE NUMBER OF FALLS
After two falls of the horse and/or competitor at obstacles during the Steeple-chase and in the Jumping Test or after three falls of the horse and/or competitor at obstacles during the Cross-Country a competitor will be eliminated.

A competitor who has fallen twice in the Steeple-chase phase or three times in the Cross-Country phase must immediately retire. If he does not, and it can be established beyond doubt that he should be eliminated on this account he should be stopped as soon as possible and reported to the Ground Jury.

RAPPING OF HORSES AND EXERCISE AREAS
It is forbidden to rap a horse in any way and in any place before, during or after a Test or at any time during the Competition, under penalty of elimination.

The only practice obstacles that competitors may jump are those provided by the organising Committee. These obstacles may be jumped only in the direction indicated by the red and white flags.

WEIGHTS AND WEIGHING
The minimum weight to be carried in the Endurance Test of all categories of International Three-Day Events, shall be 75kg for all Senior competitors, regardless of sex. There is no weight restriction for the Dressage Test and for the Jumping Test.

Weighing In: Competitors will be weighed with, if necessary, all saddlery and equipment (less bridle) carried by the horse, at the start of Phase A, before a Steward appointed for the purpose. Competitors are responsible for providing themselves in advance with such weights as may be necessary. Failure to be weighed in front of the official Steward, and/or failure to carry at least the minimum weight, involves elimination.

Weighing Out: At the finish of Phase D (Endurance Test), competitors must dismount only, under penalty of elimination, on the order of the Steward in charge of weighing. The public will be excluded from the place appointed for weighing and the competitor shall, under penalty of elimination, have no access to any unauthorised person until he has been weighed.

PASSPORTS OF HORSES
1. Every horse entered at CCN's or CCA's in a foreign country, and all horses entered for CCI's and CCIO's Championships, regional and Olympic Games, whether at home or in foreign countries, must have an Official FEI Passport or a National Passport approved by FEI, as a means of identification and to establish ownership.
2. Horses taking part in CCF's, CCA's and in competitions limited to horses from the host nation in CCI's, or at CCI's where no foreign horses are taking part, are not required to have a passport. All such horses must be properly registered and, unless there is no national requirement for vaccination in the host country and in the country or origin, all horses must have a valid vaccination certificate.

MARKING AND CALCULATION OF SCORES
1. Marking
Judges will award good marks from 0-10 for each numbered movement and for each of the collective marks.

Errors of Course or omissions will be penalised as follows:
1st Time ....2 points
2nd Time.......4 points
3rd Time ....8 points
4th Time ....Elimination

2. Calculation
2.1 The good marks from 0-10 awarded by each judge to a competitor for each numbered movement of the Dressage Test together with the collective marks are added together.

The average good marks are obtained by adding together the good marks for each judge and dividing by the number of judges.
2.2 Penalty Points
The average of good marks is then subtracted from the maximum good marks obtainable (240) in order to convert good marks into penalty points for each competition and this total is multiplied by 0.6. Any penalty points for errors of course are then added and the final total is multiplied by the chosen Multiplying Factor.
3. Multiplying Factor
The Dressage scores of all competitors will be multiplied by a Multiplying Factor to enable the Dressage scores to exert the appropriate influence on the result of the whole Competition. The Multiplying Factor will vary between 0.5 and 1.5.
3.1 If the conditions of the Endurance Test are thought to be such that few of the average competitors taking part are likely to incur penalties at the obstacles, a Multiplying Factor of 0.5 should be applied.

SADDLERY
1. The following are compulsory: An English saddle and, either a double bridle with cavesson noseband ie bit and bridoon with curb chain; lipstrap and rubber or leather cover for curb chain are optional, or a snaffle made in metal, leather, rubber or plastic material with a cavesson noseband, dropped noseband, crossed noseband or flash noseband, all made entirely of leather. A breast plate may be used.
2. Martingales, any kind of gadgets (such as bearing, side, running or balancing reins etc), any kind of boots or bandages, bit guards and any form of blinkers, fly shields, nose covers and seat covers are, under penalty of elimination, strictly forbidden. However, under exceptional circumstances, fly shields may be permitted by the Ground Jury.

PERMITTED BITS FOR DRESSAGE
Various Bridoon Bits:
1. Ordinary bridoon bit
2. Bridoon bit with two joints
3. Egg–Butt bridoon bit
4. Bridoon bit with cheeks
Various Types of Curb Bits:
5. Half-moon curb bit

6. Curb bit with curved cheeks and port
7. Curb bit with loops for lipstrap on the cheeks and with port
8. Curb bit with port and sliding mouthpiece (Weymouth)
9. Curb chain
10. Lipstrap
11. Rubber cover for curb chain
12. Leather cover for curb chain
In addition, the following types of snaffle are permitted:
13. Ordinary snaffle with double-jointed mouthpiece
14. Ordinary snaffle with jointed mouthpiece
15. Racing snaffle
16. Egg-butt snaffle:
    a) with cheeks;
    b) without cheeks
17. Other type of snaffle with cheeks
18. Snaffle with upper cheeks only
19. Rubber or leather snaffle jointed or unjointed
20. Unjointed snaffle

OBSTACLES
Double, Treble or Multiple Obstacles
1. If two or more obstacles, although sited close together, are designed as separate problems, each will be numbered and judged independently. A competitor may refuse twice at each obstacle without incurring elimination but he must not, under penalty of elimination, retake any obstacle which he has already jumped.
2. If any obstacle, although formed of several elements, such as banks or steps, any form of double, treble or multiple obstacle, placed too close together to re-negotiate each element, in the event of a refusal, it is designed as one obstacle and marked with one number but each element will bear a different letter (A, B, C, etc). A competitor may refuse only twice in all without incurring elimination but if he refuses at any part, he is at liberty to retake the obstacle or any part thereof. If, in order to retake the obstacle or any part thereof, it necessitates the competitor passing through the flags of an element the wrong way, he may do so.

THE PENALTY ZONES
1. The Penalty Zone is an area in which the horse and rider will be penalised for a fall, circle, refusal or run-out. It must not restrict the horse's room to manoeuvre as he negotiates the obstacles. If, in exceptional circumstances, it does so restrict, then the Technical Delegate or the Ground Jury have the right to extend it.
2. In the case of a single obstacle on the Steeple-Chase and the Cross-Country course, the Penalty Zone extends 10m before and 20m beyond the obstacle. It extends to a width of 10m from the boundary flags marking the limits of the obstacle. In the case of combination or multiple obstacles on the Cross-Country course, where the Penalty Zones overlap, the zone extends continuously from 10m before the first obstacle to 20m beyond

the last obstacle, or at any of the points at which a competitor might reasonably attempt to negotiate the obstacle. The limits of the Zone on either side will follow the track of the course throughout extending 10m on each side of the boundary flags marking the limits for the obstacles concerned.

The Zone will be marked for the guidance of the Jump Judge with pegs, chalk, sawdust or any other means of clear demarcation which in no way obstructs the competitor.

3. Falls, disobediences etc where they occur outside the Penalty Zone are not penalised. Any such falls do not count in the number beyond which a competitor is eliminated.

4. Having entered the Penalty Zone, a competitor must remain in the Zone until he has jumped the last obstacle within the Zone. Leaving the Penalty Zone without having jumped the obstacle(s) is penalised by 20 penalties, but this is not considered as a disobedience counting towards the number which entails elimination. A competitor is penalised for leaving the Penalty Zone, if his horse, with all four feet, has been over the limits of that zone. After incurring penalties for a refusal, run-out, circle or fall, a competitor may leave the Penalty Zone without further penalty to negotiate that obstacle.

5. Errors are penalised only when they occur within the Penalty Zone of the obstacle being negotiated. After a competitor has negotiated a single obstacle or the last of a series of elements and/or obstacles where the Penalty Zones overlap, he may circle within the Penalty Zone or leave and re-enter the Penalty Zone without penalty.

6. Competitors must negotiate a series of elements and/or obstacles in direct sequence, without bypassing subsequent obstacles or elements in order to reduce the difficulty of the obstacle(s) or series of elements. Otherwise the competitor is penalised as for a circle or a run-out.

7. Steps must be taken to ensure that no spectator is within the Penalty Zone and that no Official is in such a position as to obstruct the competitor.

PENALTIES FOR FAULTS AT OBSTACLES FOR SPEED AND ENDURANCE

Faults which occur within the Penalty Zone of an obstacle on the Steeple-Chase or Cross-Country are penalised as follows:

Disobediences:

First refusal, run-out or circle .... 20 penalties
Second refusal, run-out or circle
at the same obstacle .... 40 penalties
Third refusal, run-out or circle
at the same obstacle .... Elimination

Falls:

Fall of horse and/or rider .... 60 penalties
Second fall of horse and/or rider
on the Steeple-Chase .... Elimination
Third fall of horse and/or rider
on the Cross-Country .... Elimination

Miscellaneous:
Leaving the Penalty Zone without
jumping the obstacle, except after
a refusal, run–out, circle or fall .... 20 penalties
Error of course not rectified:
Omission of obstacle or boundary flag
Retaking an obstacle already jumped   Elimination
Jumping an obstacle in the wrong order

DEFINITION OF REFUSAL, RUN–OUT, CIRCLE AND FALLS
1. Refusal
1.1 A horse is considered to have refused if it stops in front of the obstacle to be jumped. A stop, followed immediately by a standing jump is not penalised. The horse may step sideways but if the horse steps back even a single pace, voluntarily or not, or if the halt is prolonged, this constitutes a refusal.
1.2 If a horse that has already stepped back once, is re-presented at the obstacle and halts or steps back a second time, or if the halt is prolonged and the competitor redoubles or changes his efforts, still without success, this constitutes a second refusal and so on.
2. Run-Out
A horse is considered to have run–out if, having entered the Penalty Zone and having been presented at the obstacle, it avoids the obstacle to be jumped:
a) by running out to one side or the other or b) by going to jump it at another place or c) by bypassing it deliberately in order to reduce the difficulty of the obviously offered possibilities of negotiation.
3. Circle
3.1 A horse is considered to have circled if it crosses its original track from whichever direction within the Penalty Zone.
3.2 However it is not counted as a circle when the competitor crosses his orginal track in order to make another attempt, after having been penalised for a refusal, run–out or fall. Only the refusal and/or fall are penalised.
4. Fall of Competitor
A competitor is considered to have fallen when, in the Penalty Zone, he is separated from his horse, which does not fall, in such a way as to necessitate remounting or vaulting into the saddle.
5. Fall of Horse
A horse is considered to have fallen when, in the Penalty Zone, at the same time both the shoulder and quarters have touched either the ground or the obstacle and ground.

COMPETITOR IN DIFFICULTY AT AN OBSTACLE
1. Any competitor in difficulty before an obstacle, who is about to be overtaken by a following competitor, must quickly clear the way following the instructions of the judge at the obstacle. Wilful obstruction of an overtaking competitor is penalised by elimination. A competitor eliminated for any reason must leave the course at once and has no right to

continue. A competitor catching up another may overtake only at a safe and suitable place. In such circumstances the leading competitor must give way. It is forbidden under penalty of elimination for either competitor wilfully to obstruct or cause any danger to the other.

When the leading competitor is committed to jumping an obstacle, a following competitor may only jump that obstacle in such a way that will cause no inconvenience or danger to either.

2. If in attempting to negotiate an obstacle a horse should be trapped in such a way that it is liable to injure itself or be unable to proceed without assistance, the Jump Judge shall decide if parts of the obstacle shall be dismantled or if any other assistance shall be given to extricate the horse.

3. In such a case, the Jump Judge will first instruct the competitor to dismount. The competitor is penalised as for a refusal and for a fall and must, in any case, retake the obstacle.

UNAUTHORISED ASSISTANCE

1. Any intervention by a third party, whether solicited or not, with the object of facilitating the task of the competitor or of helping his horse, is considered unauthorised assistance and the competitor is liable to be eliminated.

Exceptions

a) After a fall, or if a competitor dismounts, he may be assisted to catch his horse, to adjust his saddlery, to remount or be handed any part of his saddlery or equipment while he is dismounted or after he has remounted.

b) Whip, headgear or spectacles may be handed to a competitor without dismounting.

c) At the start of Phase B (Steeple-Chase) and of Phase D (Cross-Country) as well as at a point to be determined and announced by the Organising Committee, it is permitted to assist the competitor and to attend to his horse (groom, water etc).

PENALTIES FOR FAULTS AT OBSTACLES IN SHOW JUMPING

Knocking down an obstacle, foot in the
water or on the lath............................5 penalties
First disobedience............................10 penalties
Second disobedience in the whole test....20 penalties
Third disobedience in the whole test.....Elimination
First fall of the horse and/or competitor..30 penalties
Jumping an obstacle in the wrong order..Elimination
Error of course not rectified................Elimination
Second fall of horse and/or competitor..Elimination

As I have already said, it is extremely important that you fully understand the rules under which you are competing – at no matter what level.

COMMON INJURIES AND AILMENTS

Unfortunately there are always a few unexpected mishaps along the way. Some may not be serious in themselves but can lead on to bigger problems if not treated straight away. Remember that, under most rules, certain substances are banned from competitions so you have to keep this in mind when evaluating how best to treat the horse. The vet will inform you anyway, if he has been called in, but for minor injuries you need to be very careful about using some proprietry brands within 10 days of competing.

Sore backs

This should not happen if you have been paying proper attention to your horse's welfare, but there are times when a slight rub is barely noticeable until it reaches a certain point when just a little more serious work, such as extra sitting trot when practising flat work, can cause a very sore spot. Treat the initial soreness with mild soap and water to remove any sweat or grease from the area and, if possible, leave it open to the air. Do not rub. Once the soreness has gone apply a spirit to harden up the skin. If the sore has appeared on only one side of the back, question why and try to eliminate the cause. Are you sitting straight in the saddle? Is the saddle fitting correctly? Is the horse's back alright or is he compensating for something, and throwing more weight to the one side? A back specialist should be called in if you suspect this. Check up on and sort out any of the other problems.

Get a 'jelly pad' or surgical numnah to use once the horse is better, and keep off his back until the vulnerable area is fully healed. He will have to be lunged or turned out for exercise during this time.

Bruised foot

This is a maddening but common hazard which can happen at any time. The horse simply treads on a sharp object and bruises, or worse punctures, the sole of the foot. As the hoof cannot expand, pressure builds up and at times the horse can be very lame or just a bit 'off'.

Generally the foot will have a hot spot somewhere or a strong pulse to the area, indicating a problem, but exactly where this lies can be very difficult to determine. Bruises may clear up by themselves or develop into abscesses. Hot tubbing and poulticing will be necessary and usually the shoe will need to be removed until the soreness has worn off. It may be sensible to have pads on in order to allow the area to settle down and harden up after this sort of injury.

191

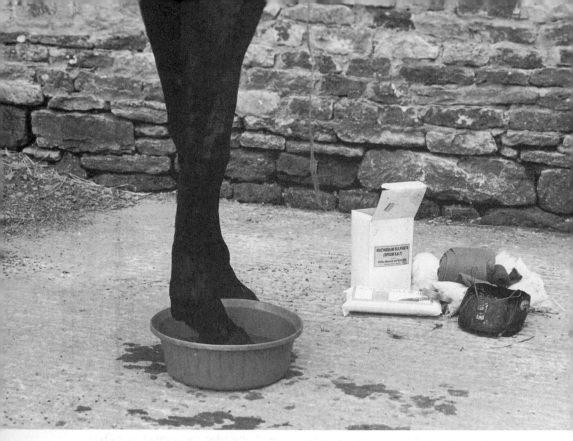

Tubbing the foot is a common treatment for bruised soles or to help 'draw' abscesses. Keep replenishing the bowl with hot water. The addition of Epsom salts helps accentuate the action. The poultice can be applied after this, and the foot well bandaged to hold it in place. The equi-boot can be useful to keep a poultice in position or for exercising a horse who does not have a shoe on

Tendon injuries

These are the injuries everyone dreads. A strain to a tendon is a serious injury requiring time to heal and then a period of hardening before the horse can resume work. Depending on the severity of the injury, this may vary from six weeks to twelve months. If the tendon is only bruised, however, for example by a blow or knock, the outlook is much brighter and, once the symptoms subside, the horse can usually resume normal work.

For any tendon injury, be it a strain or a bruise, the immediate treatment must be to prevent further injury. Ice packs applied immediately will help to minimise further damage. If ice is not available, at least a cold water bandage is necessary, firmly to give support. Keep this as cold as possible or cold–hose the leg for 10 minutes every hour until the vet arrives, and keep the horse as still as possible.

Colic

Colic can flare up unexpectedly and is usually associated with a sudden change of diet, water or, sometimes, environment. Stress has been known to give a horse spasmodic colic and it is not uncommon for colic to present itself on arrival at, or soon after, an event. Many factors contribute to this, not least a long journey, sudden cold drinks after a journey or gorging of feed, sudden excitements as well as worms, overfeeding etc.

The important thing is to prevent the horse lying down or rolling, which could cause a twisted gut. Walking quietly generally helps, particularly if it is a stress type of colic or caused by a blockage in the gut. The vet will want to know when the horse last staled or passed any dung, and whether you have heard any bowel sounds. Call the vet immediately if you do not see any signs of improvement after 20 minutes walking.

Virus

Until you really stress your horse, one of the most difficult conditions to determine is often whether he is suffering from a virus. He may show obvious signs of listlessness, going off his feed and having a temperature which is easy to see and treat, but he may on the other hand seem fine outwardly and, only when you go to a competition or for a gallop, do you feel that he is not working as well as usual or find that he gets tired very early on, starts to blow hard and, in some bad cases, gets distressed around the course.

It is imperative not to push a horse in this state but to pull up quickly, loosen the girths and get him back to the box and stables before you strain the heart or lungs. Take his temperature, which will be up anyway after exertion, but then keep an eye on it to see that it comes down as the horse cools. If you are worried that your horse does not seem right, call the vet and ask for a blood test. Treat symptoms as they arise and don't overwork the horse until you are sure he is over whatever bug he had. The milder cases are very difficult to assess, but treat any unusual loss of vigour with suspicion. On the other hand, don't let your horse pull your leg; he may be trying out your sympathetic nature!

Tying up/azoturia

This is an unfortunate condition whereby the horse's muscles, particularly those on the quarters, go into spasm. The horse often sweats profusely and starts to stiffen behind – this may spread to the whole body in bad cases. Keep the horse warm and still as movement will increase damage to the muscles. The full causes of this condition, also known as Setfast or Monday morning disease, are still unclear but it is known to be associated with overfeeding, sudden exertion after a day off, and dehydration.

In hot climates, it is fairly common for horses to 'tie up' during the 10 minute halt. A blood test must be taken to ascertain the degree of muscle damage and then proceed as guided by your vet.

Discuss your feeding routine and work programme with the vet to see if these could be affecting the horse's condition. Try to ensure that your horse never stands in throughout the day and remember always to cut food down when the horse has an easy day and never to overfeed. This is one of the most common problems in the horse world and is probably the most important single factor to affect numerous different conditions. Think fit not fat for the competition horse.

Heat stress and dehydration

Never get caught out by the effect the weather can have on your horse. Eventing is a tough sport, and hot weather and fast work will soon dehydrate your horse if you are not careful. Offer frequent drinks with electrolytes in hot weather; keep a free flow of air through the horsebox with all doors and windows open; park in the shade if possible. If the horse is sweating, wash him down frequently. Clip your horse out if he is carrying a thick coat. All these little things help to prevent unnecessary suffering.

Know the signs of heat stress and dehydration: high temperature, pinched nostrils and sunken eyes, dry skin that is slow to return to normal when pinched, and rapid breathing. These problems can be relieved with frequent short drinks as already mentioned, cold sponging, ice packs applied to prominent arteries and iced towels placed around the poll, the use of fans, etc. In very hot weather there is bound to be a certain amount of dehydration but it is up to you to be sensible and aware, and not to overdo your horse in such conditions.

Cuts and bruises

These are common to every stable and inevitably happen at some stage. Each injury should be treated, thoroughly cleaned and cared for until it has cleared up. Remember prevention is better than cure and leg protection is a wise precaution especially when galloping, jumping and doing any serious schooling on the flat.

Conclusion

It is to be hoped that the reader will have gained enough information from this book to be able to compete in horse trials through from pre-novice levels to advanced, including a three-day event. How far you will go and how well you will get on is anyone's guess because, at the end of the day, despite the training, help and general build-up necessary for competing, it is the attitude of the rider and the will to win which will get you around the courses. If you haven't the willpower or cannot take the ups and downs, the disappointments, and criticism and build on what you learn from these, you are unlikely to get far but may still have quite a bit of fun doing a sport which is essentially an outdoor one, with man's best friend, the horse, often in particularly pleasant surroundings.

The really determined rider can, however, with dedication, hard work, the will to win and learn and, of course, that essential ingredient of a talented and willing horse, aim high and go far. The opportunities are there, the rewards endless and, as a fulfilling and enjoyable sport, I can recommend none more highly.

Further Reading and Useful Addresses

British Horse Society Equitation (Country Life, 1982)

Bromily, Mary. *Equine Injury and Therapy* (Blackwell Scientific Publications, 1987)

Gordon-Watson, Mary. *Course Design and Construction* (Threshold Books, 1987)

Green, Lucinda. *Cross-country Riding* (Pelham Books, 1986)

Hedlund, Gunner. *This is Riding* (Threshold Books, 1981)

Holderness–Roddam, Jane. *Competitive Riding* (Salamander, 1988)

Houghton-Brown, Jeremy, and Powell-Smith, Vincent. *Horse and Stable Management* (Collins, 1984)

Loriston-Clarke, Jennie. *The Complete Guide to Dressage* (Stanley Paul, 1987)

O'Connor, Sally. *Practical Eventing* (Whillet & Shappeson, 1980)

Paolman, Anton. *Training Showjumpers* (J. A. Allen, 1978)

Pilliner, Sarah. *Getting Horses Fit* (Collins, 1986)

Rippon, Angela. *Mark Phillips: The Man and His Horses* (David & Charles, 1982)

Rose, Mary. *The Event Rider's Notebook* (Harrap, 1984)

Thelwall, Jane. *The Less than Perfect Horse* (Methuen, 1987)

Tuke, Diana. *Getting your Horse Fit* (J. A. Allen, 1977)

Wynmalen, Henry. *Dressage* (A. & C. Black, 1953)

Wynmalen, Henry. *Equitation* (A. & C. Black, 1938)

Xenophon. *The Art of Horsemanship* (J. A. Allen, 1962)

British Horse Society (BHS)
British Equestrian Centre
Stoneleigh, Kenilworth, Warwickshire CV8 2LR
United States Equestrian Team (USET)
Gladstone, New Jersey 07934, USA
United States Combined Training Association
292 Bridge Street, S. Hamilton, Mass 01982–1497, USA
American Horse Shows Association
220 East 42nd Street, New York, NY 10017, USA

Index

Ailments:
  back, 191
  bruised foot, 191
  colic, 193
  cuts and bruises, 194
  dehydration, 194
  tendon, 192
  virus, 193
Azoturia, 193-4

Back injuries, 191
Bandages, 123
Banks, 94-5
Barley, 27
Bedding, 33-4
  paper, 34
  shavings, 33
  straw, 33
Bits, 78-9
Boots, 108-9, 123
Bran, 27
Bruised foot, 191

Canter work, 62-4
Chaff, 27
Circles, 49-51
Clipping, 40-1
Colic, 193
Combinations, 97-101
Competing, 64, 112-28
Concours Complet Internationale
  (CCI), 16
Conformation, 18-19
Corners, 97
Counter canter, 54
Courses, 75-87
  walking, 87
Cross country, 21-2, 89-107, 112-27
  banks, 94-5

combinations, 97-105
corners, 97
ditches, 93-4
equipment, 108-11
speed, 107
spreads, 91
steps, 95-7
three-day event, 157-61
time, 142
uprights, 90-1
water, 101-5
Cuts and bruises, 194

Dehydration, 194
Ditches, 93-4
Dressage, 54, 58-61, 119-20, 129-40,
  137-8, 155-7
  marks, 137-8

Electrolytes, 31, 157
Engagement, 132
Equipment, 112-15, 156-7
Eventing, 13

Falls, 165-9, 171, 184-5
Fast work, 62-4
Feeding, 26-33, 149
Feet, 20
  shoeing, 149
Final inspection, 161
  show jumping, 161-3
Fitness, 44-68
  fast work, 62
  interval training, 64
  rider, 142-3
  swimming, 67
Flying changes, 80
Forehand, on the, 130

Grids, 72–4
Grooming, 39

Half halt, 52
Half pass, 55
Halt, 52–3
Hay, 31–3
Horse, 17
  breeding, 18
  conformation, 18–19
  movement, 19
Horse inspection, 154–5
Hydroponics, 33

Injuries, 191–4
  azoturia, 193–4
  back, 191
  bruised foot, 191
  colic, 193
  cuts and bruises, 194
  dehydration, 194
  tendon, 192
  virus, 193
International Equestrian Federation
  (FEI), 16
Interval training, 64, 148

Jumping, 21–2, 68–87
  angles, 86
  coloured fences, 74–5
  courses, 75–80
  flying changes, 80
  grids, 72–4
  improvement, 140–2
  landing, 84–6
  loose, 80–1
  lungeing, 80–1
  obstacles, 187
  strides and distances, 76–7
  trotting poles, 68–71

Lateral work, 55
Legs, 37–8
  bandages, 123
  boots, 108–9, 123
  swelling, 38
  wounds, 38
Linseed, 30

Loading, 182–3
Loops, 51
Loose schooling, 80–1
Lungeing, 80–1

Maize, 27
Market Harborough, 79
Martingales, 79
Molasses, 30
Movement, 19–20

Napping, 176–7
Nosebands, 78

Oats, 27
One-day event, 13
Over bending, 129–30

Paper bedding, 34
Passports, 185
Penalties, 188–90
Penalty zone, 187–8
Pony Club, 11

Quarters–in, 136

Rearing, 175–6
Refusal, 169
Registration, 15
Rein back, 53–4
Related distance, 76
Renvers, 55
Roads and tracks, 145, 151–3, 158
Rugs, 41–3
Rules, 15, 184–90

Saddlery, 108–9, 186–7
Salt, 31
Salute, 52–3
Schooling, 21–2, 48–62
Scoring, 185–6, 188–9
Serpentines, 53
Shavings bedding, 33
Shoeing, 37, 149
Show jumping, 120–2
  three-day event, 161–3
Slow work, 44–8
Speed, 107

Spreads, 91
Star system, 16
Steeplechase, 145–6, 158
Steps, 95–7
Stiffness, 130–2
Straightness, 132–6
Straw bedding, 33
Strides and distances, 76–7
Studs, 36
Sugarbeet, 27
Suppling exercises, 49–51
Swimming, 67, 148

Tack and equipment, 108–11
Teeth, 25–6
    wolf teeth, 26
Tendon injuries, 191
Ten–minute halt, 159–60
Three–day event, 14–15, 143–64
    cross–country, 157–61
    dressage, 155–7
    final inspection, 161
    horse inspection, 154–5
    information and briefing, 150–3
    preparation, 148–50
    roads and tracks, 145
    steeplechase, 145–6
    Ten minute halt, 159–60
    weighing–in, 160
Tiger traps, 93

Timing, 142, 158–9
Training, 21–2
Transitions, 54–5
Transport, 22
Travelling, 115–17, 181–2
    loading, 182–3
Travers, 55
Trotting poles, 68–71
Two–day event, 13

United States, 12–13
Uprights, 90–1

Vaccinations, 15–16, 40
Ventilation, stable, 35
Vetting, 20–1
Virus, 193

Walking, fitness, 44–8
Walking the course, 87
    cross–country, 105–6, 118, 151–3
    show jumping, 162
Water jumps, 101–5, 171–4
Weighing–in, 160, 185
Weights, 110–11, 185
Wolf teeth, 26
Worming, 24–5, 149

Young riders, 15

DAVID & CHARLES' EQUESTRIAN TITLES

Behaviour Problems in Horses · Susan McBane
Champion Horses and Ponies · Pamela Macgregor-Morris
Clarissa Strachan's Young Event Horse · Clarissa Strachan
Dressage Begin the Right Way · Lockie Richards
Effective Horse and Pony Management   A Failsafe System
    · Susan McBane
Equine Fitness   The Care and Training of The Athletic Horse
    · Dr David Snow and Colin Vogel
Going the Distance A Manual of Long-Distance Riding · Sue
    Parslow
Great Horsemen of the World· Guy Wathen
The Great Hunts · Alastair Jackson
Gymkhana! · Lesley Eccles and Linda Burgess
The Heavy Horse Manual · Nick Rayner and Keith Chivers
The Horse and The Law · Donald Cassell
Horse Breeding · Peter Rossdale
The Horse's Health from A to Z An Equine Veterinary
    Dictionary (new edition) · Peter Rossdale and Susan M.
    Wreford
The Horse Owner's Handbook · Monty Mortimer
The Horse Rider's Handbook · Monty Mortimer
Hunting An Introductory Handbook · R. W. F. Poole
The Imperial Horse The Saga of the Lipizzaners · Hans-
    Heinrich Isenbart and Emil Buhrer
Keeping a Horse Outdoors · Susan McBane
Lungeing The Horse and Rider · Sheila Inderwick
A Passion for Ponies · John and Francesca Bullock
Practical Dressage · Jane Kidd
Practical Showing · Nigel Hollings
Practical Showjumping · Peter Churchill
The Riding Instructor's Handbook · Monty Mortimer
The Stable Veterinary Handbook · Colin J. Vogel
Will to Win How One Young Rider Reached the Top · Rachel
    Hunt